Strategic Processing in Education

While there are certainly numerous influences on individuals' learning and performance, cognitive strategies are the processes most directly related to making meaningful progress on a learning task or problem. Written by a leading expert on strategic processing, this book situates the topic within the broader context of educational psychology research and theory and brings it to a wider audience. With chapters on the fundamentals of domain-general and domain-specific strategies, connections to other constructs, and advice for instructing students, this concise volume is designed for any education course that includes learning or study strategies in the curriculum. It will be indispensable for student researchers and both pre- and in-service teachers.

Daniel L. Dinsmore is Associate Professor of Educational Psychology in the Department of Foundations & Secondary Education at the University of North Florida, USA.

Ed Psych Insights

Series Editor: Patricia A. Alexander

Assessment of Student Achievement
Gavin T.L. Brown

Self-Efficacy and Future Goals in Education
Barbara A. Greene

Self-Regulation in Education
Jeffrey A. Greene

Strategic Processing in Education
Daniel L. Dinsmore

Cognition in Education
Matthew T. McCrudden and Danielle S. McNamara

Emotions at School
Reinhard Pekrun, Krista R. Muis, Anne C. Frenzel, and Thomas Goetz

Teacher Expectations in Education
Christine Rubie-Davies

Classroom Discussions in Education
Edited by P. Karen Murphy

DANIEL L. DINSMORE

Strategic Processing in Education

NEW YORK AND LONDON

First published 2018
by Routledge
711 Third Avenue, New York, NY 10017

and by Routledge
2 Park Square, Milton Park, Abingdon, Oxon, OX14 4RN

Routledge is an imprint of the Taylor & Francis Group, an informa business

© 2018 Taylor & Francis

The right of Daniel L. Dinsmore to be identified as author of this work has been asserted by him in accordance with sections 77 and 78 of the Copyright, Designs and Patents Act 1988.

All rights reserved. No part of this book may be reprinted or reproduced or utilised in any form or by any electronic, mechanical, or other means, now known or hereafter invented, including photocopying and recording, or in any information storage or retrieval system, without permission in writing from the publishers.

Trademark notice: Product or corporate names may be trademarks or registered trademarks, and are used only for identification and explanation without intent to infringe.

Library of Congress Cataloging-in-Publication Data
A catalog record for this book has been requested

ISBN: 978-1-138-20176-7 (hbk)
ISBN: 978-1-138-20177-4 (pbk)
ISBN: 978-1-315-50573-2 (ebk)

Typeset in Joanna MT
by Apex CoVantage, LLC

Contents

Preface		vii
Acknowledgments		ix
Introduction		x

PART I:	THE NATURE OF STRATEGIC PROCESSING	1
One:	What Is Strategic Processing?	3
Two:	Types of Strategies	9
Three:	The Development of Strategic Processing	15
Four:	Domain-General Study and Learning Strategies	24

PART II:	STRATEGIC PROCESSING IN ACADEMIC DOMAINS	37
Five:	Reading Strategies	39
Six:	Writing Strategies	52
Seven:	Mathematical Strategies	65

Eight:	Science Strategies	80
Nine:	Social Studies Strategies	92

PART III:	**NURTURING STRATEGIC PROCESSING**	**99**
Ten:	Influences on Strategy Use	101
Eleven:	Measuring and Evaluating Strategy Use	108
Twelve:	Instructional Principles to Enhance Strategy Use	117

Glossary	129
References	139
Index	153

Preface

This book is positioned as part of the Ed Psych Insights, which is intended to be written in language common to all scholars of Education and readable by the intelligent public. Rather than offering an extensive literature review on strategic processing, this particular book is designed to give readers a basic working knowledge of strategic processing.

The first audience that may find this book helpful are advanced undergraduate students, post-baccalaureate students, or students early in graduate school who wish to deepen their understanding of individuals' strategic processing. The particular aspects of this book that this audience may find particularly useful are the introductory material on strategic processing and the suggested additional readings. These additional readings will help this audience further expand their knowledge beyond what can be presented in a book such as this one. Additionally, Chapters 10 and 11, which discuss the influences of other constructs on strategy use and the measurement of strategy use, will give these readers insight into some of the bigger issues at play in the extant research literature.

The second audience that may find this book helpful are teachers or parents with some background in teaching and learning who wish to apply findings from the research literature into their educational practice, whether that be for the students in their classroom or their own children at home. To aid in the practical application of these findings, there are vignettes that begin most chapters and specific examples of strategy use throughout each chapter. These readers might find Chapter 4—domain-general strategies, the chapter on domain-specific strategies in their subject area, and Chapter 12, which discusses instructional principles, particularly useful.

Acknowledgments

There are many people who had a hand in helping me develop the ideas and writing in this book. The first of these is Patricia A. Alexander. Patricia was instrumental in shaping my ideas about educational psychology more generally, and strategic processing more specifically. Her mentorship and friendship have expanded my thinking in ways I had never anticipated. I am truly proud to be a part of the Alexander family. I was also fortunate to have two book reviewers, Luke K. Fryer and Rayne A. Sperling, whose insights and critical comments improved the manuscript immensely from its initial draft. The additional help of Jeffrey A. Greene in his role as a sounding board for some of the initial drafts of the book as well as motivational support during the writing process was invaluable to me. Finally, I wish to thank the editor from Routledge on this series, Daniel Schwartz, for helping me navigate the process of writing a book such as this. His quick and often humorous responses made the publication process for this book enjoyable.

Introduction

When thinking about the words *strategies* or *strategic*, many different situations might come to mind. Perhaps thinking about a country's strategic geopolitical goals or a corporation's strategic plan might arise, or perhaps thinking about strategies that people apply in their everyday lives—maybe being strategic in trying to get someone else in the household to do the dishes. What each of these situations has in common is that individuals or groups are employing purposeful, conscious processes to try to achieve some goal—whether that is solving a particular problem (e.g., a mathematics word problem) or learning something new (e.g., why the pull of gravity differs on Earth versus the Moon). In this book, strategic processing will be explored in many different academic domains in both formal and informal settings.

The first question is why strategic processing merits a book in an educational series such as this. While there are certainly numerous other influences on individuals' learning and performance, cognitive strategies are the processes most directly related to making meaningful progress on a learning task or problem. As an analogical example, consider the building of a house. The raw materials, plan for the house, and management of all the workers have to be in place for that house to get built. However, without the workers who employ the specific building processes—for example, nailing together the joists and framing of the house—the finished house would not exist. Similarly, the cognitive strategies individuals employ to solve problems or learn about topics have to be present for that knowledge to be built or a particular problem to be solved.

To explicate the importance of this process and how these cognitive processes work, this book is organized into three parts. Part I is a general introduction to what strategies are (and are not), what attributes of strategies are important to consider, and how strategies develop over time. Additionally, specific strategies are discussed that can be used across many contexts and situations (i.e., **domain-general strategies**). Part II discusses strategies that are more geared toward a specific domain (i.e., **domain-specific strategies**). The academic domains that are considered in the book are reading, writing, mathematics, science, and social studies. Part III discusses methods to measure strategic processing, other influences on strategic processing, and how measures and other influences on strategic processing can help teachers or instructors facilitate strategy use.

Many of the chapters include a short vignette at the beginning to help orient the reader to a practical situation in which strategies could be used. These vignettes are used to illustrate some key points and strategies throughout many of the chapters. Finally, further readings are offered as a way to extend some of the concepts introduced in this book. These are either seminal writings in that particular topic or literature reviews of that particular topic that allow the reader a more in-depth understanding of that topic. Each APA-style reference is accompanied by a short description of that reading.

Part I
The Nature of Strategic Processing

One

What Is Strategic Processing?

Jo, a first grader, looks carefully at a mathematics word problem in front of her. The problem is as follows: "If Cindy takes 5 apples from Joan, who had 10, and Richard takes 3 apples from Jeff, who had 7, how many total apples do Richard and Joan have left?" Jo decides that she first needs to use subtraction to figure out how many apples Joan and Jeff have separately. She does not remember what 10 minus 5 is, so she starts at 10 and counts backwards by five using her fingers to track how many times she needs to count back, "10 . . . 9 . . . 8 . . . 7 . . . 6 . . . 5." She repeats this counting-back procedure for the next problem, 7 minus 3 and comes up with 4. Finally, she confirms this solution by trying to remember 7 minus 3. Without even thinking she says that Joan and Jeff have 9 apples left total.

In the preceding vignette, Jo engages numerous processes to help her solve the mathematics word problem. While some of these activities are indeed strategic—the focus of this book—not all of her actions would fall under what all researchers consider as strategic. In the research literature, many authors have argued for making a clear distinction between *skillful behavior* and *strategic behavior*.[1,2]

STRATEGIES

Specifically, **strategies** are a special form of procedural knowledge (i.e., knowledge that helps someone know *how* to do something)[1] that are purposeful, intentional, effortful, used to acquire new knowledge, transfer knowledge to other problems, or transform the current problem. Going back to the vignette with Jo, she engaged in a number of different actions that conform to this definition of strategic. First, Jo engaged in a count-back strategy, using her fingers and counting back in order to subtract. What makes this process strategic in the view of many researchers in this case is that it was purposeful and effortful. In other words, she had to consciously invoke this strategy; it did not just happen without thinking about it—there was some planning or control of strategy use. Second, she consciously used a retrieval strategy for the second subtraction problem to check if the first strategy was successful. Given these two strategies, one could say that Jo was engaging in strategic processing during this problem. However, not all of her actions were strategic.

SKILLS

Some of Jo's actions were skillful. **Skills** are a special form of procedural knowledge that are automatic, habitual, effortless, and used to make progress on a given problem or learning task—such as memorizing a list of spelling words or writing an email, but not used to apply new knowledge or transform the problem in any way.[1] An example of skillful behavior in the vignette was Jo's use of retrieval for the final addition portion of the word problem. She did not have to consciously employ this retrieval process via a planning or control process, rather it was automatic. While she certainly could have employed a more effortful strategy to add those two numbers, being skillful allowed her to more efficiently solve the problem with less cognitive resources. The relation between skills and strategies can be quite complex, a topic that needs to be further explicated.

THE USE OF SKILLS AND STRATEGIES DURING PROBLEM SOLVING AND DOMAIN LEARNING

While care has been taken to differentiate the two constructs of skills and strategies, it is important to note that there are also some similarities between them. Both skills and strategies must be learned, are acquired and develop over time, and are necessary for successful problem solving and for further learning in an academic domain or making progress on solving a problem.

First, both skills and strategies must be learned. We do not come pre-programmed with a set of skills and strategies from birth—another way to say this is that skills and strategies are not innate. Rather, skills and strategies must be carefully fostered by teachers, parents, or a more knowledgeable other during learning. Think about a young child trying to tie their shoes. At first, a parent or teacher may instruct the child to use a specific strategy, such as the bunny method by crossing their laces into an "X" and pulling one lace through to make the bunny's head. The bunny ears are made by making one loop, letting it lay (the first bunny ear), making the second loop and letting it lay (the second bunny ear), then crossing the ears and pulling them together to finally tie the shoe laces together. For anyone that has spent time in a first- or second-grade classroom—or with their own children—this does not just happen without any facilitation. Eventually, the child no longer has to think about making a bunny to tie their shoes. In other words, as adults, tying shoes happens skillfully, whereas for children it is strategic. Specific teaching strategies for fostering strategic processing in learners is discussed in depth in Chapter 12.

Second, both skills and strategies are acquired and develop over time. Individuals do not learn a set of skills or strategies all at once; rather, they learn them bit by bit. For example, a child learning to swing a bat to hit a baseball typically does not start by having a 90-mile-per-hour fastball thrown toward them. Rather, the ball is typically placed on top of a stationary tee so the child can develop the skills and strategies necessary to properly swing the bat before having to anticipate the ball's arrival from the pitcher and determine the location of the ball (e.g., inside the plate, outside the plate, or right over the plate). At first, actions such as making sure the bat is parallel with the ground as it approaches the ball are effortful and purposeful. However, a major league baseball player does not need to consciously think about keeping the bat parallel; this is now skillful behavior. Rather, as an experienced hitter, a major league baseball player is being effortful and intentional in trying to predict the pitcher's next pitch. They are still being strategic, however, the strategies are aimed at more complex and advanced tasks from that of the child simply trying to swing the bat in a parallel plane. One could imagine this same scenario with a young reader who is working hard trying to decode new words that eventually become habitual for an older reader. As skills in reading increase—decoding and interpreting as two examples—readers can turn to more complex processes strategically, such as arguing with a persuasive text. The development of strategies is discussed in depth in Chapter 3.

Third, both skills and strategies are required for students to continue to acquire more knowledge and better problem solving in an academic domain. Take a moment to consider a problem-solving or learning situation that involved only skillful or strategic behavior but not both. The following problem can be used to exemplify the use of both skillful and strategic behaviors:

> In the right triangle shown in Figure 1.1, what is the measurement of the third side, labeled "x"?

What Is Strategic Processing? 7

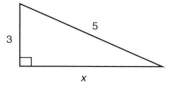

Figure 1.1 Sample geometry problem

The steps of this particular problem could encompass skillful behavior, strategic behavior, or a combination of both. Someone well versed in Pythagoras's theorem ($c^2 = a^2 + b^2$, where c stands for the side opposite the right angle and a and b stand for the remaining two sides) might immediately recognize this as a 3:4:5 right triangle and not need to employ any strategies at all—thus it is entirely skillful. Both the recognition of the problem and retrieval of the answer are automatic. A learner less well versed in Pythagoras's theorem may likely have to employ some strategies. Perhaps they consciously invoke the formula and substitute the known values in the equation for sides c and a. Following this, they solve for the remaining side, b, by squaring 3 and 5 and subtracting 9 from 25. Efficiency in solving this problem are greatly increased the more these processes are automatized—thus, both strategic and skillful behaviors are present in their processing. This allows the learner to focus on the new processes (i.e., invoking Pythagoras's theorem), rather than employing effort to do basic arithmetic. While it would be possible to do all of these processes consciously and effortfully, this would be rather tedious, particularly with a higher quantity of problems to solve or more complex problems than the one presented here.

On the other hand, imagine someone who only employed automatized skills and never used strategies. While they could certainly solve problems quickly, it would be unlikely they would be able to solve new problems, learn new concepts, or transfer concepts to other types of problems. For instance, if asked to calculate the angle of a ladder leaning against a wall (which would form a right triangle), given the distance between the wall and the ladder, skillfully applying Pythagoras's theorem would not be particularly helpful (and certainly not efficient). Rather, a learner could apply a new strategy that uses the *sine function* to calculate that angle. This would enable the learner to understand not only about the relations of sides in a right triangle but expand their understanding to the special relations among angles in a right triangle as well.

For the remainder of this book, the focus will specifically be on strategic behavior, however, one should keep in mind the importance of automatizing these processes—making them skillful—as an individual becomes a better problem solver or learner in a given academic domain.

ADDITIONAL READINGS

Alexander, P.A., Graham, S., & Harris, K. (1998). A perspective on strategy research: Progress and prospects. *Educational Psychology Review*, 10, 129–154.

This article addresses—among other things—the difference between skills and strategies and how these two constructed have, or typically have not, been conceptualized and operationalized in the extant research literature. The article also summarizes the state of the art toward the end of the last century of research on strategy use and strategy training.

Novick, L.R., & Bassok, M. (2005). Problem solving. In K.J. Holyoak & R.G. Morrison (Eds.), *The Cambridge handbook of thinking and reasoning* (pp. 321–350). New York: Cambridge University Press.

This handbook chapter is a good primer on problem solving, taking the reader through problem representation, generating problem solutions, problem search, problem-solvers' knowledge, among other topics. Most of the chapter is a domain-general treatment of problem solving, however, there is some attention specifically paid toward problem solving in mathematics.

Two
Types of Strategies

Lee is sitting at his lab bench in chemistry class with an unknown acidic solution (analyte) in a flask. His instructions are to figure out what the concentration of that acidic solution is, given the amount of impure acid dissolved in the water in the flask as well as the concentration of a base solution (titrant) that has also been provided. He first underlines the important values in the written text of the problem that was left on the lab bench. Before beginning, Lee decides to add a pH indicator—bromthymol blue in this case. He then proceeds to use a pipette (an instrument to transfer liquid from one container to another) to slowly add the titrant to the analyte, until the analyte changes color. He then repeats this process three more times in order to be more precise in the amount of titrant needed to create a permanent color change in the analyte.

Now that strategies have been explicitly defined in Chapter 1, a discussion of the different types of strategies described in the literature is in order. At the broadest level, researchers have described three main types of strategies—cognitive, metacognitive, and epistemic strategies.[3]

Cognitive strategies are those strategies that are invoked to actually solve a problem or learn more about a topic[1]—in other words, these strategies are the ones that actually accomplish specific tasks and goals the learner has. These are the strategies that were exemplified in Chapter 1 and will be the focus for the rest of this book. Lee engaged in numerous cognitive strategies while trying to solve the acid concentration problem in the vignette, including underlining and titrating. **Metacognitive strategies** are those that are aimed at monitoring or controlling the cognitive strategies that have been employed.[4] For instance, one might decide that the cognitive strategy employed was ineffective, such as deciding to reread a passage and still not understanding it. Additionally, one then might decide on a new strategy, such as looking up words they do not know in the dictionary. Finally, **epistemic strategies** are those that are aimed at reflecting on the limits, certainty, and criteria of knowing,[3] which may influence both an individual's cognitive and metacognitive strategies. For instance, when deciding whether or not to believe that climate change is caused by human factors—factors such as emitting carbon dioxide into the atmosphere by burning fossil fuels—a person may ask themselves what criteria (e.g., evidence) would be necessary to support such a belief. More detailed descriptions of metacognitive and epistemic strategies are discussed in two other books in the Innovation Series and are listed at the conclusion of this chapter in the *Additional Readings* section.

DOMAIN-GENERAL AND DOMAIN-SPECIFIC STRATEGIES

Cognitive strategies have been divided further into either domain-general or domain-specific strategies. Before the distinction between domain general and domain specific is discussed, it is important to be explicit about what is meant by the term *domain*—specifically academic domains. Academic domains refer to particular fields of study, such as physics or history. **Domain-general strategies**, then, are those strategies that can be employed effectively in any task, regardless of the academic domain.[1] For instance, using a sorting or categorizing strategy would be considered domain-general strategy use. When Lee underlined the important terms and amounts in the written problem in the vignette, he was employing a domain-general strategy—a strategy that would work both in the vignette and in other tasks, such as reading about the US Civil War in the domain of history. Domain-general strategies are discussed in more detail in Chapter 4.

Domain-specific strategies are those strategies that can only be employed effectively in a particular domain.[1] For instance, when Lee chose to add a titrant to the analytic, he was employing a domain-specific strategy because titration would be ineffective in other domains such as writing or historical inquiry. Domain-specific strategies in reading, writing, mathematics, science, and history are discussed in more detail in Part II. However, as will be evident in those chapters, some strategies do not always fit neatly within one category or the other—particularly in the domains of science (Chapter 8) and social studies (Chapter 9).

DEEP-LEVEL AND SURFACE-LEVEL STRATEGIES

Another way researchers have differentiated cognitive strategy types is by level. Marton and Säljö were the first to describe how different types of task questions would elicit different levels of processing, levels they named surface-processing and deep-processing.[5,6] **Surface-level strategies** are those strategies that are aimed at trying to understand the problem or task.[7] For example, Lee's use of underlining in the vignette would be described as surface level in addition to domain general. Lee was not trying to transform the problem, rather just trying to understand what he should do to solve it or understanding what the problem is asking. On the other hand, **deep-level strategies** are those strategies that involve a more

12 The Nature of Strategic Processing

extensive manipulation or transformation of a task or text.[7] Lee's use of titration in the vignette would be described as deep level because he is changing the parameters of the problem (specifically the acidity of the solution) to learn what the concentration of acid was in the original flask.

Around the same time that Marton and Säljö were conducting their experiments, Craik and colleagues investigated ways in which individuals memorized information (rather than reading comprehension in Marton and Säljö's case), also describing memorization processes along a surface- and deep-level continuum.[8] In situations where individuals were simply trying to memorize information through a rote process, individuals would be described as using surface-level strategies, such as rehearsing (i.e., repeating the information to themselves multiple times). However, in situations where the individual sees the information as relevant to them, pays a lot of attention to the information, and has enough prior knowledge about the topic, they may display more deep-level strategies, such as connecting the new information to what they already know.

These two initial frameworks are not the only ones to classify strategies in this way, though. One example of a different approach to this problem is Biggs's Approaches to Learning that also described different types of processing. In Biggs's Approaches to Learning, he theorized three types of processing: reproducing (which is analogous to surface-level processing), internalizing (analogous to deep-level processing), and organizing (analogous to metacognitive processing) approaches.[9]

The primary difference between the frameworks proposed by Marton and Säljö and Craik and Lockhart versus Biggs are that those frameworks proposed by the former group of researchers theorized processing to be relatively unstable over the learning task (i.e., state based), while the latter group of researchers theorized that processing would be relatively stable over learning tasks (i.e., trait based). **Trait-based** frameworks would predict that the types of strategies an individual employs over their schooling would be relatively stable, particularly across shorter periods of time, regardless of the task at hand. For example, if we gave Lee a task such as memorizing the atomic numbers in the periodic table of elements, a trait-based framework would predict that Lee would use similar types of strategies in all of the tasks he has been asked to do.

On the contrary, **state-based** frameworks would predict that strategy use would vary as a function of the task at hand. If we again asked Lee to memorize the atomic numbers of the periodic table, we would expect that because the nature of the task differs, he would employ different strategies. The expectation here is that he would employ primarily surface-level strategies (such as rehearsal), rather than employ any of the deep-level strategies he used in the vignette. In the next chapter, two state-based frameworks are described in terms of how strategic processing may develop (i.e., change) over the course of time and tasks attributes.

ADDITIONAL READINGS

Niaz, M. (1994). Enhancing thinking skills—domain specific/domain general strategies: A dilemma for science education. *Instructional Science*, 22, 413–422.

Differentiates and provides a framework for domain-specific versus domain-general strategies. This article also provides numerous examples of these types of strategies in the domain of science as well as tying these cognitive strategies to metacognitive strategies.

Dinsmore, D. L., & Alexander, P. A. (2012). A critical discussion of deep and surface processing: What it means, how it is measured, the role of context, and model specification. *Educational Psychology Review*, 24, 499–567. doi:10.1007/s10648-012-9198-7

14 **The Nature of Strategic Processing**

This systematic literature review examines contemporary studies on the relation of surface- and deep-level strategies to task outcomes. The article describes possible relations between levels of processing and performance that are quite mixed including the conceptualization of surface- and deep-level processing, measurement of strategic processing, and current model of levels of processing.

Greene, J. A. (2018). Self-regulation in education. New York: Routledge.

This text, also in the Innovations Series, takes a more in-depth look at metacognitive and self-regulatory processing.

Three

The Development of Strategic Processing

Margaret is a precocious young reader. As a 12-year-old she picks up Othello *and begins to read it. Although she is a good reader, she finds part of Shakespeare's play rather difficult to understand. When she feels like she does not understand something in the play, she tries many different things to better understand that part of the text. For instance, as she reads Roderigo's line, "What a full fortune does the thicklips owe if he can carry't thus!," she first tries to remember if she has seen some of those words before. When that does not work, she reads the sentence again in its entirety. Finally, Margaret decides to move on to other parts of the text to see if these other pieces of text will help her understand Roderigo's line.*

As a college undergraduate studying English literature, Margaret again picks up Othello. *Now as she reads the text there are very few areas of the text in which she needs to think about whether she understands the play and very few strategies she needs to employ as she reads it. Unlike before, Margaret can usually choose a strategy that works the first time, or not need to think consciously about understanding the text at all.*

This chapter addresses the development of strategic processing over time. Two frameworks will be used to describe changes in strategy use. The first framework, Overlapping Waves Theory, described changes in children's strategy use and has primarily been used with younger children. The second framework, the Model of Domain Learning, described changes to individuals' strategy use as they develop expertise in an academic domain and has mostly been used with adolescent and adult learners.

OVERLAPPING WAVES THEORY

Siegler and Jenkins described Overlapping Waves Theory (OWT) as part of a broader developmental framework similar to Piaget's developmental framework.[10] With regard to strategies in this framework, OWT proposed three major principles: that individuals use a variety of strategies, that the use of a lot of different strategies is typical, and that strategy use changes as a result of experience.[10] First, the notion that children use multiple strategies to solve problems is an important one because it is often assumed that children are not strategic or rely on one way to solve a problem. In fact, reports of children's strategy use, particularly in mathematics, has shown that not only do children use multiple strategies, but they often have primary and backup strategies.[11] In the vignette, 12-year old Margaret actually employed multiple strategies—accessing her prior knowledge, rereading, and connecting to an other text. Second, strategies change as a result of the experiences and tasks that children and adults encounter in their everyday lives, similar to Piaget's notion of the equilibration of knowledge.[12] Thus, what children experience can help determine how their strategy use changes over time.

The next mechanism that OWT proposed was that children acquire strategies over long periods of time; more effective strategies win out over less effective strategies; the choice of which strategy to use becomes increasingly adaptive; and there is an increased efficiency in strategy use over time.[10] First, Siegler and Jenkins stressed the developmental nature

The Development of Strategic Processing 17

of strategy use by noting that only through repeated experiences over time do we acquire new strategies. It is unlikely that we would be able to acquire a strategy well enough with just one or two exposures. One could imagine that *Othello* was not the only Shakespearian play that Margaret had read, and that those other plays would influence her strategy use while reading *Othello*.

Second, learners do not always use or retain strategies that they have previously acquired. In other words, strategies that might have been helpful once may be replaced by an even better strategy in the future. Think of it as a sports team where there can only be so many players on the roster. As new players are added, some players have to be let go. This is graphically represented in Chen and Siegler's figure showing the "waves" of strategy use.

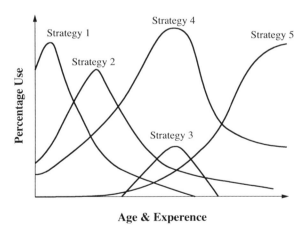

Figure 3.1 Chen and Siegler's "waves" of strategy use
From Chen & Siegler (2000). Reprinted with permission.

One can imagine that as Margaret gets older her rereading strategy fades as she learns new reading strategies such as relying on contextual clues to figure out specific words—like "thicklips." Additionally, learners get better at determining which strategies will work better over time—which strategies they should keep and which strategies they should no longer use. Another way to say this is that there is a concurrent change in cognitive strategy use as the learner improves their metacognitive strategy use—their ability to monitor and control their own cognitive strategy use. As monitoring and control processes improve, learners can select better strategies that are more likely to work.

This in turn leads to an increased efficiency over time in strategy use. For example, in mathematics, finger counting (also referred to as dactylonomy) in and of itself is not a bad strategy, and indeed may have many positive benefits beyond simply solving the problem.[13] However, finger counting is relatively inefficient, as it is more time-consuming than simply retrieving an addend from memory. During a relatively complex mathematics problem that involves fractions, having to continually count on one's fingers would increase the time to solve the problem, and more importantly, could increase the likelihood of making a mistake if cognitive resources were used for inefficient strategies or skills, such as finger counting, rather than more efficient strategies or skills, such as retrieval.

THE MODEL OF DOMAIN LEARNING

While Alexander's Model of Domain Learning (MDL) addressed strategic processing, it is important to note that the MDL described changes to strategic processing in the context of other important changes—namely prior knowledge and

The Development of Strategic Processing

interest. The components of the model will be discussed first, followed by the stages of expertise, and finally a discussion of how strategic processing changes over time.

According to the MDL, the three components to developing expertise in a given academic domain are knowledge, interest, and strategic processing.[14] Knowledge comes in two forms—domain knowledge and topic knowledge. **Domain knowledge** refers to the breadth and scope of subject-matter knowledge.[15] For instance, knowing the major principles of archaeology and how to properly excavate different types of historical sites would be domain knowledge in archaeology. **Topic knowledge** refers to the depth of knowledge about a specific content related to a domain.[15] For instance, knowing many facts about the ancient sanctuary in Delphi, Greece would be an example of topic knowledge in archaeology. Interest also comes in two forms—individual interest and situational interest. **Individual interest** refers to students' sustained disposition toward a topic or content area.[16] For instance, a teenager who likes to take apart every mechanical device she sees to understand how it works would have individual interest for engineering. **Situational interest** refers to externally triggered, task-specific interest.[16] For instance, another teenager may only be interested in how her smartphone works, thus there may be little individual interest in engineering, but high situational interest for the specific topic of how smartphones work. Hidi and Renninger described how situational interest can turn into longer term individual interest over time.[16]

Along with strategic processing, knowledge and interest are hypothesized to change over the course of the journey toward expertise, unlike many previous models of expertise that simply specified a number of hours necessary to become an expert.[17] The MDL proposed that learners go through three different stages on their quest toward expertise in a domain. In each of the stages—acclimation, competence, and proficiency—learners are theorized to have distinct levels and combinations of knowledge, interest, and strategies. Briefly, as individuals progress from acclimation to proficiency, levels of domain and topic knowledge are expected to increase.[14] More importantly, though, this knowledge is expected to become less fragmented and more interconnected.[18] Similar to domain and topic knowledge, individual interest is expected to increase during the development of expertise, however, reliance on situational interest is expected to decrease.[18] While situational interest is expected to decrease, it plays an important role in strategic processing, particularly in acclimation.

Specifically, with regard to strategic processing, there are myriad changes in how individuals employ specific strategies. These changes have to do with the quantity, type, and usefulness of the strategies employed. First, similar to knowledge and interest, there are changes to the frequency of strategy use. However, it is not the case that all types of strategies increase. Specifically, it is predicted that deep-level strategies should *increase* from acclimation to proficiency, while surface-level strategies should *decrease* from acclimation to proficiency.[18] This relation is graphically depicted in Alexander's figure, which follows.

These changes in surface- and deep-level strategies may happen for two important reasons. The first is related to changes in the individual's knowledge from acclimation to proficiency. As discussed before, individuals gain more domain and topic knowledge in addition to that knowledge being more cohesive. In acclimation, when knowledge is fragmented, it would be difficult for someone to use deep-level strategies such as

The Development of Strategic Processing 21

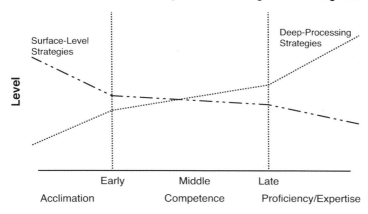

Figure 3.2 Changes in strategic processing as predicted by the Model of Domain Learning
From Alexander (2004). Reprinted with permission.

connecting knowledge. If there is little cohesion in the existing knowledge, there is little to connect to. In the vignette, one reason Margaret may have been able to more easily apply strategies would be that she had a lot more cohesive domain knowledge about English literature. This may include knowledge about specific vocabulary typical for those types of texts.

The second reason for the change in surface- and deep-level strategies is the tasks that individuals may engage in during proficiency versus acclimation. An acclimated learner is likely to be engaged in tasks that have correct and incorrect answers and may be well structured. **Well-structured tasks** are tasks that have one correct answer and a specific or a few specific ways to achieve that correct answer.[19] On the other hand, those in proficiency are tasked with creating new knowledge and developing questions to explore unknown frontiers in the domain. These tasks that someone in proficiency would be engaging in may not have a correct answer and may be ill structured. ***Ill-structured tasks*** are tasks that do not have a correct answer and may have numerous ways to achieve an answer to the posed question—in other words, they are not well structured.[19]

In addition to the change in surface- versus deep-level strategies, there may be changes with the other types of strategies discussed in Chapter 2, domain-general and domain-specific strategies. There are again two reasons for this, the first reason related again to their storehouses of knowledge. Because acclimated learners do not possess much breadth or depth of knowledge, they will have very few domain-specific strategies at their disposal, because these rely on domain knowledge. Thus, these learners in acclimation must rely heavily on their domain-general strategies instead.[14] During the progression to proficiency as knowledge increases, there should be a resulting increase in domain-specific strategies as breadth and depth of knowledge grows. However, it should be noted that as one spends more time in the academic domain, there would be an expectation that those domain-specific strategies become routinized and therefore skillful rather than strategic[14] (refer back to Chapter 1 to the discussion on skills versus strategies).

Finally, besides the frequency and type of strategies employed, the usefulness of the strategies employed is also an important consideration. Using a strategy—whether deep level, surface level, domain specific, or domain general—does not guarantee that the strategy will ultimately be helpful in solving a given problem or generating new knowledge. Imagine a child or adolescent reading about black holes for the first time, with little prior knowledge, and trying to use a visualizing strategy (trying to form a mental picture) to understand the text. Without the requisite domain and topic knowledge to form this mental picture, it is unlikely that any visualization

The Development of Strategic Processing

would help. Rather, there might be other strategies, such as referring back to previous portions of the text, that might be more helpful.

In terms of this quality of strategic processing, Alexander hypothesized that the competence stage would be a "period of optimal strategy use" (what Siegler and Jenkins called increased efficiency), because learners were using surface-level and metacognitive strategies more efficiently, gaining domain-specific strategies, and engaging in tasks that are both new and complex enough to use those strategies effectively.[14] In the vignette, Margaret as a younger reader clearly struggled to use strategies efficiently and effectively, while as an undergraduate, she was able to employ strategies she knew would work. Suffice it to say that the development of strategy use over time is not necessarily a straightforward or linear process.

ADDITIONAL READINGS

Siegler, R.S., & Jenkins, E.A. (1989). *How children discover new strategies*. New York: Psychology Press.

This book describes how children's strategy use develops over a period of time based on their individual learning experiences. The book is an outcome of a series of lectures that Siegler gave and is based on his past work with Jenkins. The book expounds on the four mechanisms of strategy development discussed in this chapter, among other topics.

Alexander, P.A. (2004). A model of domain learning: Reinterpreting expertise as a multidimensional, multistage process. In D.Y. Dai & R.J. Sternberg (Eds.), *Motivation, emotion, and cognition: Integrative perspectives on intellectual functioning and development* (pp. 273–298). Mahwah, NJ: Lawrence Erlbaum Associates.

This book chapter is an updated exposition of the Model of Domain Learning from the initial 1997 description. The chapter goes into more detail about the components of expertise development (knowledge, interest, and strategies) as well as the developmental stages of expertise (acclimation, competence, and proficiency).

Four

Domain-General Study and Learning Strategies

Mary is studying for a history test about the role of explorers in the 15th and 16th centuries, a topic she did not know a lot about before studying. She is trying to memorize the explorers' names and which area of the globe that particular explorer was most active in. She reads the textbook chapter on explorers and underlines each of the explorers she thinks is going to be on the test. Additionally, she makes flash cards with the explorers' names on the front of the card and the area of the globe they explored on the back. For example, she writes, "Vasco da Gama" on the front of one flashcard and "India" on the back. She does well on the test, but remembers little of the information she studied a week after the test.

As described in Chapter 2, **domain-general strategies** refer to those strategies that one can use to be successful in any domain. These strategies can be used across many different learning and study situations. While there are numerous different definitions of what learning is, **learning** is often defined as a change in one's mental schema—that is, both what the person knows and how their knowledge is organized.[12] For example, in the vignette, learning would be instantiated as either Mary adding more facts to her existing schema or changing her schema about the role of explorers in history. For the former instance, she could add to her schema that Vasco da Gama was the first European to sail to India. For the latter instance, she might modify her schema that Europeans discovered the American continent. Instead of thinking that Europeans discovered the Americas, she might begin to understand that there was a complex relationship between European explorers and the indigenous peoples that inhabited the Americas before the Europeans' arrival.

Studying, like learning, also has numerous definitions and is a bit harder to define. In fact, Winne and Hadwin called studying a "fuzzy task."[20] Some definitions of studying are very similar to definitions of learning, while other definitions simply define studying as preparation for a test. In the context of this book, **studying** is defined as any sort of cognitive engagement that the learner uses to perform better on a task or test they are about to take.[21] Unlike learning, studying may or may not result in any long-term changes to an individual's schema. In the vignette, Mary's studying—reading the text and using flashcards—had some short-term benefit but little long-term benefit.

Now that learning and studying have been explicitly defined, a more comprehensive examination of domain-general learning and study strategies is in order, including how these domain-specific strategies might develop over time. Domain-general strategies have been categorized into six different categories for the purpose of this exploration: attentional strategies, organizational strategies, elaborative strategies, working memory strategies, generative strategies, and help-seeking strategies.

ATTENTIONAL STRATEGIES

The first category includes strategies that help individuals attend to important information. These include strategies such as underlining and highlighting that are used as surface-level strategies to try to understand important information, typically in text. **Underlining** and **highlighting** are very common study strategies that individuals use. Typically, underlining and highlighting are useful in marking important information that the person will go back and study again (often paired with other strategies such as rehearsal, discussed later in the chapter). However, underlining and highlighting have only been shown to be effective in limited circumstances.[22] Generally, underlining and highlighting have been shown to be useful to memorize lists or terms for shorter time periods—an upcoming test, for example. In addition to being domain-general strategies, underlining and highlighting are also considered surface-level strategies, because these strategies do not transform the problem in any way; rather, they are just used to better understand the problem. In text, for example, they are often used to remember the main points or important details—something Mary did in the vignette that enabled her to do well on her test.

ORGANIZATIONAL STRATEGIES

Organizational strategies, on the other hand, do not necessarily fit neatly into the surface versus deep distinction. Some organizational strategies are more surface-level processing, such as notetaking, while others could be considered more deep-level processing, such as concept mapping.

Notetaking is a relatively common strategy, but instead of being used to attend to information like highlighting or underlining, it is used to organize information. One particular issue with the strategy of notetaking is that it can be hard to define, because how individuals take notes and what they decide to take notes on can vary from person to person. Notetaking can occur during a variety of activities including reading, listening to a lecture, or watching a video. Similar to underlining and highlighting, notetaking is considered a surface-level strategy to understand the task or problem. Again, similar to underlining and highlighting, notetaking only seems to be effective in certain situations. Specifically, notetaking seems to be more effective for those individuals that have less prior knowledge about the content they are taking notes on,[23] although the research on this topic is somewhat mixed.[24] For example, because Mary did not previously know a lot about explorers, she might benefit greatly from notetaking, whereas another student who knew a lot about explorers from a previous learning situation would likely not benefit as much.

Outlining is an organized way for an individual to list concepts and related subordinate concepts (details about the main concept) in an explicit manner. Outlines can take many forms and have a variety of levels to represent subordinate concepts. Similar to highlighting and underlining, outlines are a process used to isolate the most important information. However, unlike highlighting and underlining, outlines enable an individual to show hierarchical relations (an arrangement in order of importance or rank) between information.[25] An example outline follows:

Schizophrenia

I. Simple
   A. % of Americans: 1/10
   B. Symptoms: Gradual withdrawal and disinterest in the world
   C. Severity: Most likely to fend for themselves

II. Paranoid
   A. % of Americans: 1
   B. Symptoms: Feeling of being persecuted
   C. Severity: May live in a marginal way

III. Catatonic
   A. % of Americans: 1/10
   B. Symptoms: Peculiar motor behavior alternating between stupor and frenzy
   C. Severity: Series of short attacks over many years

IV. Hebephrenic
   A. % of Americans: 3/4
   B. Symptoms: Regressive behavior and total disregard for personal hygiene
   C. Severity: Most severe

Figure 4.1 An example outline for the topic of schizophrenia
From Robinson and Kiewra (1995). Reprinted with permission.

While outlines can be useful to show hierarchies within a concept and details related to that concept, individuals cannot show linear relations between concepts with an outline.[26] Graphic organizers, on the other hand, can convey other types of meaningful information that outlines cannot. **Graphic organizers** use spatial relations to show how different concepts are related in a linear or non-linear manner. Non-linear relations could be depicted using matrices or tree diagrams. An example of a matrix about the same topic as the outline shown previously, schizophrenia, might look like this:

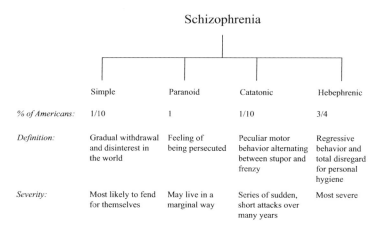

Figure 4.2 An example graphic organizer for the topic of schizophrenia
From Robinson and Kiewra (1995). Reprinted with permission.

Interestingly, when given enough time, evidence has suggested that students were better able to apply knowledge learned through graphic organizers than outlining when they were given sufficient time to do so.[27]

Similar to graphic organizers, concept mapping is another way to organize and relate concepts to each other. **Concept maps** generally consist of a central concept, related concepts, linkages between those related concepts using lines or arrows, and propositions that describe those relations.[28] Concept maps were first predominately used in science learning, but have since been extended to many different academic domains. For example, there may be a central concept in the map which is "concept maps," related concepts such as "linking words," linkages between those concepts (i.e., a line), and finally, the linkage is described with a proposition "have."

While concept maps have the potential to enable individuals to represent complex relations in a manner they can construct or generate for themselves, having enough prior knowledge to be able to construct a usable concept map is often challenging.[29]

ELABORATIVE STRATEGIES

Elaborative strategies include mnemonics, method of loci, self-questioning, and self-explanation. These are considered deeper-level strategies that enable an individual to gain new knowledge or transform a task or problem. **Mnemonics** are memory strategies that provide some sort of meaningful organization of new knowledge for that individual. There are many examples of mnemonics, which include acronyms (using the first letter of each word in series to easily retrieve it), method of loci (using spatial memory by creating a mental spatial map such as a street layout and matching an item to one of those spatial markers), keyword methods (imagining a pot on a duck's head to remember duck in Spanish—pato),[30] and rhymes. Acronyms are among the most familiar of these mnemonics. For example, PEMDAS is an acronym for the order of operations in mathematics—parentheses, exponents, multiplication, division, addition, and subtraction.

Method of loci might also be familiar, sometimes referred to as a mind palace in popular culture such as the television show *Sherlock* on the BBC. Method of loci involves designating a series of known objects with a list of unfamiliar objects. For example, one might choose a path through their kitchen passing the sink, stove, and refrigerator as the three known objects. The order of these objects is first memorized. Then, the unknown items to be memorized are associated with those known objects—the kitchen objects. For instance, if Mary is trying to memorize the explorers Christopher Columbus, Vasco da Gama, and John Cabot, she might imagine Columbus sailing around the sink, da Gama on the hot stove (tying that to the Thar Desert in India), and Cabot in the freezer (tying that to his exploration of the cold Arctic region). Once these have been well associated, all she needs to do is remember her trip through the kitchen—sink to stove to refrigerator— to recall the list of unknown words that were Columbus, da Gama, and Cabot. These two elaborative strategies, like notetaking, tend to benefit those with lower prior knowledge more so than those with higher prior knowledge.[31] One possible explanation for this is that the connection between prior knowledge, either in a mnemonic or in the method of loci, are conceptually weak.

Self-questioning is a process whereby an individual generates their own question(s) about the task or problem (which again could be a reading, lecture, or video) and attempts to answer their own question(s). Unlike underlining, highlighting, and notetaking, the strategy of self-questioning appears to have greater benefits for long-term encoding and retention of the material being studied.[32] Additionally, evidence supports the notion that self-questioning can be even more effective than **summarizing** the material (i.e., identifying the main ideas and supporting details over time).

Similar to self-questioning, self-explanation is a strategy whereby individuals try to generate in their own words in a way to understand and integrate new knowledge from a task or problem into their own schema. **Self-explanation** is the process of producing one's own explanations about the material being studied during or after a task.[33] Given adequate levels of prior knowledge, the primary advantage to a strategy like self-explanation is that not only can it achieve better longer-term retention of the material, it has also been shown to allow individuals to use this new knowledge to solve novel (i.e., new) problems without specific prompting of the individual to do so.[34] In the vignette, although Mary remembered the information for the test using highlighting and flashcards, using self-questioning or self-explanation may have enabled her to remember the information long after the test.

WORKING MEMORY STRATEGIES

Once information has been attended to, organized, or elaborated, there are also various domain-general strategies that individuals can employ to keep that information in working memory. These strategies include rehearsal and chunking. **Rehearsal** involves repeating information to maintain that information in short-term or working memory (i.e., memory stores that have a short duration for new information that can be further processed).[35] As with other surface-level strategies in the previous categories, rehearsal has limited benefits. On the positive side, repeating information can help maintain information in short-term or working memory long enough to be further processed. However, there is no link between the amount of rehearsal and improvements in memory performance over the long term.[35] Mary's use of flashcards in the vignette, a type of rehearsal, and the resulting shorter-term retention of knowledge, would be quite typical.

In addition to rehearsal, another way to influence short-term or working memory is to use categorization processes such as **chunking**, either to retain the information in working memory or to begin to encode that information into long-term memory (i.e., relatively permanent storage of information). Chunking refers to the process of recognizing familiar patterns and rapidly encoding to or recalling from long-term memory large related chunks of information.[36] This strategy was initially examined with chess players, where master chess players (who are very good at chess) were able to rapidly recognize and recall from long-term memory intricate chess patterns that novices (who are not as good at chess) could not. In other words, a chess master could recall formations of many chess pieces very quickly with just a few clues.[37]

GENERATIVE STRATEGIES

Many of the deep-level strategies described previously enable someone to generate new knowledge or new insights into a topic using these strategies. Fiorella and Mayer recently described eight such strategies that facilitate further learning, which they call generative.[38] These generative strategies include some of the strategies previously discussed such as concept mapping, summarizing (i.e., identifying the main ideas and supporting details), drawing (i.e., creating spatial representations), self-questioning, and self-explanation. Two additional generative strategies that Fiorella and Mayer discussed are teaching and enacting. **Teaching** is explaining the material or information to someone else. **Enacting** is creating a way to "act out" the material or information.[38] For instance, instead of using a mind palace, Mary could have acted out these explorations of the explorers, using objects in her house to trace their routes across the globe.

HELP-SEEKING STRATEGIES

Help seeking is not always described as a cognitive strategy per se, rather a strategy designed to take advantage of other resources in the learning or studying environment. Thus, some describe it more as a metacognitive strategy. **Help seeking** is the strategy of identifying and using environmental resources such as technological or social assistance to improve learning or task performance. For example, an online article about a history topic may offer a glossary that the reader can click on to get a definition for a term or concept they did not previously know. These types of computer-assisted scaffolds are generally only useful if the learner possesses adequate metacognitive strategies (to monitor and control their own learning) as well as cognitive strategies that would enable them to utilize help they were given.[39] Help seeking can also occur when an individual asks someone else for help—social help seeking. As with help seeking from affordances in the environment, this strategy is more helpful when the person providing the help has to be able to provide useful information or strategies to the learner and when the learner feels like they are able to ask for help. Thus, cognition and affect can influence the use of help seeking. Learners that have low self-efficacy (who believe that they cannot do a task well) and have unsupportive teachers are much less likely to ask for help.[40]

THE DEVELOPMENT OF DOMAIN-GENERAL LEARNING AND STUDY STRATEGIES

Used in concert, these domain-general strategies can offer a powerful way for acclimated learners to gain a foothold into an academic domain for which they have little prior knowledge about or prior experience with. Many of these strategies, particularly the elaborative and generative strategies, can be helpful in connecting their existing fragmented knowledge to make a more coherent understanding of the academic domain (a topic discussed in the previous chapter).

It is important to note that just because a strategy is simple, or surface level, does not mean that strategy may be any more or less useful than a deep-level strategy.[41] For example, because Mary was new to the topic of explorers in the vignette, her initial foray into learning about explorers may rely more heavily on surface-level strategies because she may not have had enough prior knowledge to engage in deep-level strategies like elaboration. The usefulness of a given strategy may have more to do with the goal or goals of the learner than with the actual strategy itself. These goals might be cognitive goals (i.e., goals intended to help solve the problem) or metacognitive goals (i.e., goals intended to help the learner monitor or control their own processing). For example, if an individual was trying to cram for a test tomorrow, using flashcards to repeat information over and over again may be more effective and efficient in the short term. However, if that individual's goal was to build a coherent knowledge base about a certain topic and learn information to be used in the future and applied to new problems, flashcards would be neither effective nor efficient. In that case, it would be more beneficial to use a strategy such as self-explanation.

Another way to enhance domain-general strategies is to think about if and how they are paired together. With a specific goal in mind, one could imagine pairing or combining multiple domain-general strategies to reach that specific goal—a process termed bundling.[42] However, in order for this bundling to work, most research has demonstrated that this bundling has to be specifically prompted or trained—in other words, it does not just happen on its own. Specific instructional techniques for enhancing strategy use are discussed in detail in the last chapter of this book, among which some would be appropriate methods to facilitate bundling.

If used effectively, domain-general learning and study strategies have the potential to allow individuals to gain a foothold into an academic domain. However, as individuals become more engaged in a domain (i.e., move toward competence), they need to develop domain-specific strategies in those domains, which is the focus of Part II.

ADDITIONAL READINGS

Dinsmore, D.L., Grossnickle, E.M., & Dumas, D. (2017). Learning to study strategically. In R.E. Mayer & P.A. Alexander (Eds.), *Handbook of research on learning and teaching: Second edition* (pp. 207–232). New York: Routledge.

This chapter provides a systematic review of study strategies in the contemporary educational psychology literature. Evidence for the effectiveness for each of the study strategies in addition to which types of tasks these strategies are most effective for are the major focus of the article. In addition, methodologies for measuring study strategies are discussed.

Fiorella, L., & Mayer, R.E. (2015). *Learning as a generative activity: Eight learning strategies that promote understanding.* New York: Cambridge University Press.

This book discusses eight deeper-level, domain-general strategies that can help students learn new knowledge and help them apply that knowledge to new situations. Among the strategies discussed are summarizing, mapping, drawing, imagining, self-testing, self-explaining, teaching, and enacting. This book provides a more detailed overview of these types of strategies.

Robinson, D.H., & Kiewra, K.A. (1995). Visual argument: Graphic organizers are superior to outlines in improving learning from text. *Journal of Educational Psychology*, 87, 455–467.

> This article discusses the advantages and disadvantages of different types of domain-general study strategies. The study examined the nature of the graphic organizers, study material, and learning outcomes that led to their conclusion that graphic organizers were superior to outlines. Specific recommendations for the use of graphic organizers are provided.

Novak, J.D., & Cañas, A.J. (2008) The theory underlying concept maps and how to construct and use them. Technical Report. Institute for Human and Machine Cognition, Pensacola, FL.

> This technical report discusses the genesis of concept maps, their construction, and how they might be used in the assessment process. There are numerous helpful examples of concept maps as well as illustrations of how concept mapping differs in terms of learning and memory from more rote-type approaches. Finally, the report discusses the archiving of expert knowledge.

Winne, P.H., & Hadwin, A.F. (1998). Studying as self-regulated learning. In D.J. Hacker, J. Dunlosky, & A.C. Graesser (Eds.), *Metacognition in educational theory and practice* (pp. 277–304). Mahwah, NJ: Lawrence Erlbaum.

> This chapter examines the complementary role of self-regulated learning in the study process. By examining studying through a metacognitive lens, they identify four stages of studying: task definition, goal setting and planning, enacting study tactics and strategies, and metacognitively adapting studying. This chapter articulates the relations between the strategies discussed in the current chapter of this book, with another level of strategic processing—namely, the metacognitive level.

Part II
Strategic Processing in Academic Domains

Part II of this book introduces domain-specific strategies. The academic domains of reading, writing, mathematics, science, and social studies are addressed. These were mainly chosen because they are the core academic domains in schools; however, other domains in the arts and humanities would certainly be interesting areas of exploration.

Each of these chapters begins with a vignette describing strategy use in the specific academic domain that that chapter is about, a discussion of the particular strategies core to that academic domain, and followed by a more in-depth discussion of how those strategies may grow and develop over time using the lenses of Overlapping Waves Theory and the Model of Domain Learning.

Five
Reading Strategies

After watching a movie about aliens, David wonders if scientists think it is likely that extraterrestrials exist on other planets. He goes to the library and selects a book titled, Where is Everybody? Fifty Solutions to the Fermi Paradox and the Problem of Extraterrestrial Life.[43] *He carefully reads the introductory chapter, but pages through the chapter that addresses who Enrico Fermi was. However, he pays particular attention to the solutions listed in the next chapter, evidence that would support the notion that extraterrestrials exist. He carefully underlines information and takes notes. When he gets to the Zoo Scenario (that aliens exist but observe us from hidden locations), he uses his prior knowledge of seeing animals in zoos to better understand that position.*

Reading strategies have both been investigated in the research literature as strategies for reading in their own right (i.e., reading is considered its own academic domain) as well as strategies that can be used for learning about another domain (e.g., reading about a science topic such as oxidation). In the vignette, David's purpose for reading the text was to learn more about extraterrestrials rather than to practice or enjoy reading. One could imagine a different scenario where David was reading a narrative text, such as *War and Peace* for enjoyment. Although these situations differ in terms of the goals for reading, there is a similar set of reading strategies that has been reported during reading that helps readers comprehend text.

The process of reading has been defined as the interaction between reader and text.[44] In the context of reading strategies, the reader comes to the reading situation with a set of cognitive and metacognitive strategies for reading (along with other attributes like reading knowledge and topic knowledge about the text), but in addition to coming to the text with particular skills and strategies, attributes of the text also influence the use (or non-use) of those strategies. For example, David might have used re-reading as a strategy before, but if the complexity of the Fermi paradox text was sufficiently complex, he might have to employ a different strategy. Fortunately, the wide variety of strategies and reading behaviors that have been investigated are such that readers have many options to employ while strategically reading a text. The examination of reading behaviors and how these can be used strategically will be guided by a description given by Pressley and Afflerbach.[45]

One additional way to categorize reading strategies is to differentiate those that are surface level (e.g., understanding the problem) with those that are deep level (e.g., transforming the problem), a distinction described in detail in Chapter 2. For reading, surface-level and deep-level strategies have domain-specific instantiations. These distinctions between surface- and deep-level strategies have been guided by Kintsch's Construction-Integration Model (CIM).[46] The CIM described two types of processes—those aimed at the text base and those aimed at the situation model.[47] Briefly, processes aimed at the text base help the reader form a mental representation of the text—in other words, what the text is saying. Processes aimed at the situation model are those that integrate the text with the reader's prior knowledge—in other words, incorporating what is being said in the text with what the reader already knows.

SURFACE-LEVEL STRATEGIES

Pressley and Afflerbach discussed 11 cognitive strategies and two evaluative strategies that can be used to understand the text. The first two are reading aloud and rereading. **Reading aloud** is a strategy in which a reader who is reading silently begins to read a sentence or passage aloud to better understand the text. **Rereading** is a strategy of reading a fragment, sentence, passage, or text more than one time to better understand the text. While there is not a rich literature base on the effectiveness of reading aloud, there is quite a bit of research regarding rereading. Rereading, either a fragment or whole text, has shown fairly mixed benefits in terms of how well it aids in comprehension, with some studies showing many reading gains and others showing very little change in comprehension.[48,49]

Another common reading behavior is skimming. **Skimming** is skipping over portions of the text. This may include only reading some words or sentences (perhaps only bolded words or the first sentence of each paragraph). Skimming could be used non-strategically by reading random parts of the text or strategically, if the reader knows what the important parts of the text are likely to be. In the vignette, David skimmed over the chapter on Enrico Fermi by skipping large portions of the text.

At the word level, readers can use strategies to figure out the meaning of a word that they do not already know. **Guessing the meaning of a word in context** is the strategy of using the words that surround the unknown word to guess at that word's meaning. For example, if David did not know what the word "interstellar" meant, it might help to read the word in the context of a sentence such as, "First, the distances between stars that would possess planets capable of supporting life are *very* great, too great to permit interstellar travel." Because the sentence is discussing that distance between stars and the unlikeliness of traveling between them, he might infer from that sentence that interstellar means "occurring or situated between stars."

Other more word- or fragment-oriented strategies are underlining (or highlighting, which are discussed as domain-general strategies in Chapter 4) or using text features. These are both strategies aimed at trying to distinguish important information. **Underlining** text is self-explanatory; however, using text features is a bit more ambiguous. **Using a text feature** is any process by which the reader uses an organizing feature of the text (such as a heading or a table) to better understand what the author is trying to say. For example, David might have used the headings in the text to signal when the section on Enrico Fermi's life was over and the text about solutions to the Fermi paradox began.

Beyond identifying important pieces of the text, readers may want to employ strategies to help memorize parts of the text. Three such strategies could be used this way—rehearsal, local restatement, and global restatement. **Rehearsal** is the strategy of repeating parts of the text in order to retain it in memory (either in working or long-term memory). In the previous example about interstellar travel, David might want to remember what the definition of interstellar is, so he might repeat "interstellar travel is travel between stars" to himself a few times (either silently or out loud). **Local restatements** are paraphrasing or repeating text information at the microstructure level (i.e., at the sentence or paragraph level). David might restate a particular piece of the text (such as a sentence fragment) that described the zoo hypothesis for himself. **Global restatements** are paraphrasing or repeating text information at the macrostructure level (i.e., between paragraphs). For example, David might restate the chapter on the zoo scenario as describing extraterrestrials observing us but hiding their location so humans do not know they are being watched.

Finally, with regard to the surface-level cognitive strategies, there are two strategies that involve connecting parts of text together. **Making connections to prior text** is the process of recalling earlier parts of the text to help the reader understand what they are currently reading. For example, perhaps David's reading about the zoo hypothesis helped him understand a similar solution to the paradox called the *planetarium hypothesis*. **Predicting the micro or macrostructure of the text** is the processes of determining what the text is about to say. At the textbase level, this process relies on the structure of the text to enable the reader to figure out what is going to happen. Deep-level prediction will be distinguished between surface-level prediction described in a subsequent section.

In addition to these 11 surface-level strategies, there are two evaluative strategies that readers can use to better comprehend (make meaning of) a text. These are evaluating text quality and evaluating the importance of text. **Evaluating text quality** is the process of making a judgment as to the particular merit of the text itself. For example, if David noted that the author failed to correctly put some text in quotations, this evaluation might help him determine some appropriate cognitive strategies to understand that text, despite this limitation in the written text. Failure to evaluate that text quality might leave a reader confused as to what the author was intending to say. **Evaluating the importance of text** is the process of making a judgment of the relative merits of each part of the text—in other words, being able to distinguish the main ideas and supporting details from irrelevant information. Failure to evaluate what is important, especially if there are "seductive details" present, can impair a reader's ability to be strategic with what they decide to rehearse or retain from the text.[50]

DEEP-LEVEL STRATEGIES

There are eight cognitive strategies and two evaluative strategies that can be used to integrate what is in the text with a reader's own knowledge base. These strategies include predicting, making connections to background knowledge, making connections to background experience, and global restatements about the argument. **Predicting**—as a deep-level strategy—refers to using the reader's prior knowledge to predict what is going to happen next. Unlike surface-level prediction, where the reader is using the structure of the text to predict what is coming next, deep-level prediction uses prior knowledge to make the prediction, thereby integrating what the reader already knew with what was happening in the text.

Parallel to the surface-level strategies of making connections between portions of a text, there are two deep-level strategies that also are specifically about making connections. **Making connections to background knowledge** refers to using what we already know (from long-term memory) to help us understand what the text means. For example, given the passage:

> Although we have not yet seen planets like Earth in other solar systems directly, we have already inferred their existence by examining the gravitational pull that they exert on their parent stars. This gravitational pull creates a "wobble" in the parent star's visible light emissions. This wobble is referred to as the Doppler effect.[43]

A reader might better understand what the Doppler effect refers to if they recall from their prior domain knowledge that the Doppler effect is the increase or decrease in the frequency of a wave (light, sound, or otherwise). Similarly, the reader may also connect to personal experience. **Connecting to personal experience** is the process of using some past experience to help the reader understand what the text is saying. If a reader has ever heard the change in the sound waves of an ambulance or fire truck passing by, they may have noticed that the pitch of the siren is higher as it approaches and lower as it moves further away from them due to the relative proximity of the wave crest as the distance between the two objects changes. This personal experience may help the reader understand why in an analogous way scientists see light waves change as they are moving relative to the position of another planet.

There is also a deep-level corollary to the global restatement that was referenced in the surface-level processes. **Global restatements aimed at the argument** are not an attempt by the reader to make sense of the macro- and micro-structure of the text; rather it is a strategy that uses what one already knows to interpret the argument the author is making, which involves understanding the positionality of the author (what the author believes), positionality of the reader (what the reader believes), and how those two might relate. For example, David could read the text about the existence of extraterrestrial civilizations, in which the author was trying to convince the reader that extraterrestrials did not exist, however, because David did not try to globally restate the argument, he may not know this is what the author was trying to do. Perhaps his beliefs were so firmly entrenched with the notion that humans have already been abducted by aliens that he failed to see them not existing as a plausible argument, or he may have just failed to employ any deep-level strategy at all.

Unlike the strategies just discussed, some deep-level reading strategies do not have corollaries to surface-level processing. Two such strategies are arguing with text and questioning. **Arguing with text** refers to the reader refuting an argument the author has made. For instance, David might have read that:

> *Numerous studies of genetics demonstrate that all life on Earth is highly related, which some use as evidence that our DNA came from a single origin outside of Earth. For example, some studies indicate that 75% of human genes or close variants exist in worms, that we share half our genes with the banana, and that 98.4% of human DNA is similar to that of ape DNA.*[43]

He might decide that this argument does not support the notion that life on Earth was "seeded" from another planet. He might argue that while all life on Earth is highly related, that might just mean that the single origin was from Earth, not from another planet, which would refute the notion that our DNA is extraterrestrial (or alien) DNA. **Questioning** is similar to arguing with text, except that instead of raising a counterpoint, the reader asks himself or herself a question to prompt further thinking—which might lead to arguing with text or another related strategy. For instance, David might have simply asked himself, "Who knows if there is any unintelligent life on other planets?" Questioning with text is highly similar to the domain-general strategy of self-questioning discussed in Chapter 4.

Two particular deep-level strategies that require more extensive prior knowledge to be used successfully (a topic discussed again in Chapter 11) are interpreting and elaborating. **Interpreting** is reasoning with information beyond what is in the textbase to integrate that new negotiated meaning between textbase and situation model to change the reader's situation model. **Elaboration** is also reasoning with information beyond what is in the textbase, but unlike interpreting is meant to build meaning tangential (somewhat unrelated) to the text. For example, David might elaborate by thinking, "We should find extraterrestrial civilizations in the universe; the thing is so big there has to be other people out there."

Finally, with regard to deeper-level evaluative strategies, a reader could evaluate agreement or text quality about the argument. **Evaluating agreement with text** refers to a process by which the reader assesses the level of consistency between what they perceive to be the author's stance and what they perceive to be their stance on an issue. This could result in agreement or disagreement—David could think, "I also agree that there aren't any ETCs." **Evaluating the quality of the argument** refers to the process of making a judgment as to the particular merit of the argument, rather than the text itself, which was defined previously as the surface-level strategy of evaluating text quality. For example, after reading a text about extraterrestrials, David might think, "I wish the author would provide better proof to support his point that we haven't already had extraterrestrial sightings."

OTHER METACOGNITIVE AND EVALUATIVE STRATEGIES

In addition to the four evaluative strategies discussed previously, there are also other metacognitive and evaluative strategies specific to reading that are addressed more in depth in other texts in this book series on self-regulation. Depending on the theoretical lens, some of these strategies may be viewed as more evaluative, while others may be viewed as more metacognitive. These strategies include **evaluating comprehension** (i.e., did the reader understand what they just read?), **evaluating interest** (i.e., is the reader interested in what they are reading right now?), **expressing empathy** (i.e., feeling of sympathy imputed to others), **expressing surprise** (i.e., feelings of shock or bewilderment), and **expressing amusement** (i.e., feelings of enjoyment of pleasure). These metacognitive strategies that relate to either *cognitive* (with regard to the first strategy) or *affective* (with regard to the rest) dispositions of the reader can strongly influence the other metacognitive and cognitive strategies one employs.[4] For instance, feelings of empathy while reading about a Syrian child stuck in the middle of a war zone may change the cognitive processes one employs while reading the rest of that article.

DEVELOPMENT OF READING STRATEGIES

The development of reading strategies has been described at length by Alexander.[51] Her description closely followed that of her broader theoretical model, the Model of Domain Learning (MDL) that described learning in any academic domain. Her description of the development of reading followed the MDL in terms of the development of its three main components—namely knowledge, interest, and of course strategies.

First, Siegler and Jenkins's predictions about strategy use in Overlapping Waves Theory (OWT) should also apply to reading (although their framework is cited much more often in the mathematics literature).[41] Siegler and Jenkins proposed that a variety of strategy use is typical and that these strategies change as a result of experience. In examinations of strategy use through think-aloud protocols (which are

Reading Strategies 49

described in depth in Chapter 11), it is clear that children, adolescents, and young adults use a wide variety of strategies. Indeed, elementary-school students,[52] middle-school students,[53] high-school students,[54] and college undergraduates[55] use a wide variety of strategies, with few exceptions.

Using Alexander's description of reading development, a sizable percentage of the students in those studies were *effortful processors*. This profile describes students who use a lot of strategies and a wide variety of strategies, albeit with less metacognitive monitoring and control than *competent readers*, who also use a wide variety of strategy and skills, but do so in a much more efficient manner. There were also changes detected in the way that students used strategies among these age groups in those studies cited in the preceding paragraph. For example, there were shifts from the use of surface-level strategies to deep-level strategies for more competent readers (mostly as they aged), another prediction specifically derived from the MDL. Thus, changes in strategy use by the reader, the second of Siegler and Jenkins's predictions, also play out in the development of reading. Strategy use increases over time, but for competent reading to develop, this has to be accompanied by metacognitive (and possibly epistemic) strategies to ensure that the more effective and efficient strategies are used in favor of those that are less effective and less efficient.

As the MDL predicted, though, these changes in strategy use for reading do not happen in a vacuum. In addition to strategy use changing as a result of experience, which Siegler and Jenkins rightly pointed out, changes in strategy use can also come about as knowledge and interest change. Going back to the reader profiles mentioned earlier, at all levels there were students who fit *knowledge reliant* and *interest* reliant profiles. With these readers, increased strategy use only occurs for texts for which they have high levels of knowledge for the *knowledge reliant* readers or high levels of interest for the *interest reliant* readers. For the former group—the *knowledge reliant* readers—most of the strategies relate to their prior knowledge, such as connecting to background knowledge or experience. For the latter group—the *interest reliant* readers—most of the strategies they employ are evaluations of interest followed by cognitive strategy use only when those evaluations of interest for the text are positive.

However, there are exceptions to the prediction that readers will use higher quantity and variety of strategies as they get older. Two particular profiles fit this pattern of low strategy use—namely *challenged* and *resistant* readers. These two groups either do not employ strategies because they do not have the relevant knowledge to do so (for the *challenged* readers) or because they are not sufficiently motivated to do so (for the *resistant* readers). Instructional strategies to facilitate these types of readers are discussed in detail in Chapter 12.

ADDITIONAL READINGS

Alexander, P.A., & The Disciplined Reading and Learning Research Laboratory. (2012). Reading into the future: Competence for the 21st century. *Educational Psychologist, 47,* 259–280.

This article discusses what competent reading looks like in the 21st century. The authors posited a view that the nature of reading is multidimensional, goal directed, and developmental. The article uses the Model of Domain Learning as a framework to discuss among other issues processes and strategies that go hand in hand with their conception of reading development.

Pressley, M., & Afflerbach, P. (1995). *Verbal protocols of reading: The nature of constructively responsive reading.* Hillsdale, NJ: Lawrence Erlbaum Associates.

This book describes both a comprehensive list of reading behaviors upon which the current chapter is framed as well as a discussion about how to measure these behaviors.

Alexander, P. A. (2005). The path to competence: A lifespan developmental perspective on reading. *Journal of Literacy Research, 37,* 413–436.

This paper, which was commissioned by the National Reading Conference, describes a developmental model of reading based on the Model of Domain Learning. It also describes how combinations of reader attributes (which includes strategic processing) could be used to identify strengths and weaknesses in reading that may lead to comprehension success or difficulty.

Dinsmore, D. L., & Alexander, P. A. (2016). A multidimensional investigation of deep-level and surface-level processing. *Journal of Experimental Education, 84,* 213–244. doi:10.1080/00220973.2014.979126

This empirical study is an example of using the think-aloud protocol to measure individuals' strategic processing in reading. Additionally, the study examined the role that type of text as well as type of outcome question play in the relation between strategic processing and performance.

Six
Writing Strategies

Luke's assignment for history class is to write about the yellow fever epidemic that occurred in Philadelphia, Pennsylvania, in 1793. Luke first identifies some source materials to write from, some of which are primary sources (like Benjamin Rush's firsthand account of the epidemic) as well as secondary sources (like a passage from his Pennsylvania history textbook). Luke decides that he wants to focus on the African American nurses that tended to the city's ill, because he thought his teacher might appreciate the different perspective he was taking. He used an outline to figure out his main points and drew on his knowledge—having visited Philadelphia many times—to think about things in the city he could discuss in his essay. As he was writing, he kept wondering if his teacher would appreciate the points and supporting details he was using. Finally, after writing, Luke reread his essay and inserted a few additional details he thought his teacher would find interesting.

Similar to reading, writing strategies described in the research literature can help improve writing performance as well as being somewhat useful in other domains as well. For example, we see Luke looking for multiple different types of sources, a domain-specific strategy in history that will be discussed in the social studies chapter.

To organize the various strategies that people use while they write, numerous models of writing have broken the process down into smaller sub-processes. Two such models that have had a major influence in research on writing strategies are Flower and Hayes's Cognitive Process Model and Graham and Harris's POW model.

Flower and Hayes proposed four key points in their model of writing: it is a set of distinctive thinking processes that are coordinated; these thinking processes are well organized and hierarchically arranged; the thinking processes are goal directed; and writers create their own goals by developing a sense of purpose for writing and revising those goals as they write.[56] These distinctive thinking processes, which will be described in more detail subsequently, were organized further into three sub-processes: pre-write, write, and re-write, also referred to as planning, translating, and reviewing. They proposed that goals for writing are set during the planning stage and that these goals are revisited as the writer re-writes or revises their work. Finally, they proposed monitoring activities that take place during writing (metacognitive strategies) that guide an individual's thinking processes. For example, as Luke was writing and when he finished writing, he continually evaluated whether or not his ideas and supporting details would be interesting to his teacher.

Graham, Harris, and colleagues have also proposed a model of writing that has some similarities to Flower and Hayes's model. They used a mnemonic (described in Chapter 4) to help younger writers remember the steps—POW. POW stands for "pick my idea," "organize my notes," and "write and say more."[57] This is a simplified version of their previous model, with picking my idea and organizing my notes being roughly analogous to planning, and write and say more being roughly analogous to translating in Flower and Hayes's model. Most notably, Graham and colleagues have implemented strategy training along with writing models such as

POW called the Self-Regulated Strategy Development (SRSD) model.[58] This model focuses heavily on helping to enhance students' strategy use and self-regulation skills.[59]

In addition to these two general models of writing, second language writing (L2 writing) has also been a particular area of interest in the literature. While many of the strategies used by L2 learners are similar to those used in L1 (their native language) writing processes, some of these processes differ. Notably, there is the need not only to translate what is in an individual's head into written text, as in Flower and Hayes's model, but writing in a foreign language also involves translating that L2 writer's thoughts from one language to another prior to translating it into written text.[60] Thus, there is an extra step necessary for an L2 writer to accomplish the same writing task as someone writing in their native language. This may involve additional strategies, such as using a Spanish-English dictionary to translate words from their native language into the language they are currently writing in.

He and colleagues organized specific strategies that aligned with the processes of planning, translating, and revising based on Flower and Hayes's model.[56] Additionally, they added L2 and monitoring strategies that will also be briefly discussed.

MONITORING STRATEGIES

During these three stages (pre-writing, writing, and re-writing), larger metacognitive and self-regulatory strategies that guide the domain-specific writing strategies that follow, as well any domain-general strategies, may be employed. Some of these monitoring strategies are very specific to the act of writing. Examples of these writing-specific monitoring behaviors are monitoring the meaning of written words and monitoring text organization. For example, a writer might constantly monitor as they write and after they write to ensure that the cognitive strategies and skills they are employing are actually resulting in a comprehensible text.

Additionally, there are some more domain-general metacognitive strategies that a writer might engage in that includes monitoring their initial goals and evaluating the quality of each draft they write. With regard to monitoring initial goals, a writer might use their metacognitive experiences to figure out if they are reaching their metacognitive and cognitive goals for writing.[4] For instance, in the vignette Luke might draw on his past experiences writing previous essays for his teacher to better judge if his essay would be interesting to his teacher. If not, he may decide to enact some explicit domain-general strategies to help guide his future strategy use, such as self-evaluation or self-questioning as described in Chapter 4.

PLANNING STRATEGIES

Two main planning strategies will be discussed here that align with metacognitive strategies (strategies to monitor and control cognitive strategies as discussed in Chapter 2) rather than with specific cognitive strategies. However, it is important to discuss them here because they are metacognitive strategies that are germane to the process of writing. These two metacognitive strategies are organizing thoughts and ideas and identifying a potential audience.

Organizing thoughts and ideas is a planning strategy that allows a writer to develop a systematic manner in which to present their ideas for the reader based on the goals they had developed for writing. This organization can happen at both the global (organizing thoughts across many paragraphs) and local levels (organizing the flow of sentences within a paragraph). In order to implement this strategy, a writer may rely on a number of domain-general strategies for organizing that were discussed in Chapter 4. For example, outlining may be a particularly useful domain-general strategy to organize their thoughts. In the vignette, Luke used this particular strategy to outline his important points and supporting details *before* writing. A writer could also use a concept map about writing strategies to organize the complex relations between the main idea and supporting details they were writing about. In sum, during the planning phase it would be important to engage in metacognitive strategies of planning, but also employ some of the domain-general strategies to help organize those plans in some reified manner.

Not only do writers have to organize their thoughts before writing, but they also must be aware of who they are organizing those thoughts for. Another metacognitive strategy that can help a writer do this is by identifying a potential audience. **Identifying a potential audience** is the strategy of matching *who* we are writing for and *how* we are presenting our thoughts. Identifying the audience may involve taking into account factors such as the reader's interest and their level of prior knowledge about the topic being written about. For example, in the vignette Luke is carefully considering his audience (his teacher) and deciding if what he plans to write is appropriate for that audience. If Luke was writing this essay for someone else, say a pen pal, perhaps he would plan to include different main points or supporting details, especially if he knew that the pen pal did not possess the historical knowledge about Philadelphia that his teacher did. As with the organizing and planning strategies, writers might rely on a number of domain-general strategies in order to determine fit between their ideas and the interests of the audience.

TRANSLATING STRATEGIES

Once we have made a plan and ensured that that plan fits our audience, writers have to undergo the task of translating the ideas from their mind to paper or computer. He and colleagues described two general types of processes to do this, retrieval from long-term memory and reasoning processes.[60] The first two strategies they described are directly recalling propositions and activating background knowledge. **Directly recalling propositions** from long-term memory, while certainly strategic at some point, should soon become skillful in order to create more complex sentence and text structures. This process, if not quickly automatized, may make writing less efficient if writers have to consciously retrieve information as they write. An analogous example of this would be in reading. If a reader had to be conscious of their phonemic decoding, comprehending complex text would be difficult because most of the cognitive resources of the individual would need to be directed toward decoding.

Second, activating prior background knowledge of both vocabulary and word meaning (semantic awareness) can help in this translating sub-process as well. Again, similar to reading, **activating background knowledge** can be a purposeful way to retrieve meaningful information from long-term memory that assists in turning the thoughts in our mind into meaningful prose. For instance, Luke activated his background knowledge of Philadelphia in the vignette to help him provide supporting details. This may be particularly helpful because the information retrieved should be immediately accessible from long-term memory, rather than having to search through source material to find relevant supporting details.

In addition to the two translating strategies discussed earlier, writers can also use reasoning strategies to translate ideas into written discourse. Two such processes are inductive and deductive reasoning. While these can be used as more domain-general processes, these strategies are particularly salient in writing. **Inductive reasoning** is the process of using a set of particular experiences to generate a specific rule.[61] For example, Bertrand Russell famously described the inductive reasoning and the limitations of that reasoning from the viewpoint of a chicken:

> Domestic animals expect food when they see the person who usually feeds them. We know that all these rather crude expectations of uniformity are liable to be misleading. The man who has fed the chicken every day throughout its life at last wrings its neck instead, showing that more refined views as to the uniformity of nature would have been useful to the chicken . . . The mere fact that something has happened a certain number of times causes animals and men to expect that it will happen again. Thus our instincts certainly cause us to believe that the sun will rise to-morrow, but we may be in no better a position than the chicken which unexpectedly has its neck wrung.[62]

Specifically for writing, writers may use their experiences with both spoken and written word use, spelling, and grammar to decide how to translate those thoughts into the written word. For someone growing up in the North Midland region of the United States (roughly centered around Pittsburgh, Pennsylvania), the grammatical construction of the verb *need* followed by a passive participle—such as washed—is quite common (this results in phrases such as "The car needs washed").[63] Given enough experiences, writers using inductive reasoning may use these grammatical constructions quite often.

However, this is an incorrect grammatical construction, as it should be written, "The car needs *to be* washed."

While inductive reasoning uses experiences to create a grammatical rule, **deductive reasoning** is the process of using a generalized rule that has been learned.[61] Instead of constructing a grammatical proposition based on an experience, a writer would either strategically—and eventually skillfully—use deductive reasoning to construct a grammatical proposition using standard rules of English grammar. As with inductive reasoning, deductive reasoning can also lead to incorrect grammatical propositions as the English language in particular has many exceptions to those rules.[64] For example, to make the word "stop" past tense, not only does a writer have to add an "ed," they also have to add an extra "p" to the "ed" to get "stopped." Indeed, a writer might develop (or in this case follow) a new rule, that if a verb has one syllable and ends with a vowel followed by a consonant (such as "stop" or "tap"), the last consonant needs to be doubled.

REVISING STRATEGIES

Following the translating stage, strategies are also useful during the revision process. Strategies used during the revision stage that have been examined in the literature have included both those aimed at improving the clarity of writing, as well as grammar, spelling, and punctuation. The strategies of **improving grammar, spelling, and punctuation** are three such strategies that a writer could employ. For instance, if a writer had written, "The car needs washed," at the revising stage a "to be" should be added to correct his error during translation. Similarly, these changes can be made to spelling and punctuation.

Revision strategies aimed at improving the clarity of writing have been a bit more nebulous to identify in the literature.

Improving the clarity of writing can refer to improving clarity either at the global or local level (similar to the levels in planning discussed earlier in the chapter). Improving the clarity of writing at the global level might involve making sure there is a flow to the argument in a persuasive text or making sure there is alignment in the plot elements of a narrative text. For instance, during revision a writer might ensure that the events surrounding the main character in their story are in a logical chronological sequence. At the more local level, a writer might make sure one sentence logically leads into the next.

L2 STRATEGIES

The final set of strategies are specific to learners who are writing in a language other than their native language (the first language they learned), called L2 strategies or compensation strategies.[60] Three examples of L2 writing strategies are direct translation, consulting translation dictionaries, and using synonyms. The first of these, **direct translation**, is the process of directly retrieving the translated word from long-term memory. While this certainly could be strategic at first, it is quite likely that in a short period of time this should become skillful (i.e., automatic).

If that strategy fails, or is not yet available to the writer, an L2 writer may decide to **consult a dictionary** to look up the translation of a certain word. The availability of this strategy may be dependent on the environmental affordances, such as the availability of a bilingual dictionary. Fortunately, translation applications via cell phone, tablet, and computer have put these affordances more easily in reach. Finally, **using synonyms** is a strategy that L2 writers might use to substitute a synonym for either an unfamiliar or uncertain word. For instance, if a writer tries to use a more complex word like "photosynthesis," but is not sure it is the correct word (or how to spell it), they might instead write "the process of converting sunlight into energy."

DEVELOPMENT OF WRITING STRATEGIES

Unlike mathematics, which is discussed in the next chapter, much of the research on the development of writing strategies has been studied with populations that have a variety of learning disabilities. This includes much of the research framed by Graham and Harris's SRSD model, as well as other interventions such as ANSWER.[65] Despite this paucity of research in the development of writing strategies for typically developing writers, both Siegler and Jenkins's Overlapping Waves Theory (OWT) and Alexander's Model of Domain Learning (MDL) can help conceptualize optimal trajectories for strategy development in writing.

First, according to OWT, one would expect writers to rely on multiple strategies, that these strategies would change over time, and that these strategies would become more adaptive and flexible over time. Consider translating strategies as an example of multiple strategy use. Writers should engage in inductive reasoning during the translating process in order to build rules over time. However, there would be two problems with relying solely on an inductive, bottom-up process. First, there would be the chance that the rules a writer has developed were the result of experiences in which the grammar or syntax were poor, thereby developing a poor grammar rule. Second, relying solely on induction would be a relatively inefficient process to develop a set of rules, which may or may not be correct according to Standard English (or whatever dialect or language one is trying to write in). Rather, simultaneously relying on deductive reasoning (working from rules or prototypes that have been learned) as well as inductive reasoning would lead to an inductive-deductive cycle that should maximize efficiency over time.[61] Thus, multiple strategy use (here inductive and deductive reasoning) could be quite advantageous over relying on isolated strategy use.

Second, these strategies should become more adaptive and flexible over time. In other words, a writer's increasing amount of metacognitive knowledge (what a writer knows about themselves and the task) and metacognitive experiences (a writer's affect about the task) should help the writer choose strategies more appropriately.[4] For example, an L2 writer might try to decide between looking up a word in a Spanish-English dictionary to write the correct translation of the word they want, or, just use a different synonym that they know. While at first, they might solely use the former strategy because they feel more confident in it, their reliance on the synonym strategy might replace the bilingual dictionary as their metacognitive experiences change.

Finally, strategy use should develop as a function of a person's increasing expertise. Similar to how changes in metacognitive strategies should influence cognitive strategies, increases in domain knowledge, topic knowledge, individual interest, and situational interest (which were discussed in detail in Chapter 3) should also influence cognitive strategy use for writing.[18] Increases, particularly in individual interest (i.e., long-term interest), should result in increases in strategy use over the course of expertise development.[61] While situational interest (shorter-term interest) will likely not have those longer-term benefits,[14] tasks that are situationally interesting (possibly the topic of dinosaurs for young children), might have strategic benefits, at least in the short term.

Particularly as writers move toward the final stage of expertise, proficiency, some of these writing processes may begin to look very different with regard to either the types of strategies used or the amount of strategies used, and indeed expert writers might engage in very little strategy use because these cognitive processes have mostly been automated—allowing for greater processing or the use of more advanced strategies. For example, using deductive reasoning in the translation sub-process of Flower and Hayes's model might be fully skillful (at least for grammar and spelling) for the expert. This may enable them to be more strategic in ways that those in acclimation and competence may not. Going back to the example earlier of planning a clear, chronological plotline in the planning section, an expert may not rely on chronology, but rather create a non-linear timeline in the plot as a writing tool to engage the reader. Many books and movies have used flashbacks that were used to develop characters and create suspense, as in many of the *Arabian Nights* tales and in the television show *Lost*. Those with greater expertise may be able to use these strategies with greater effect than those with less domain-specific knowledge and interest.

ADDITIONAL READINGS

Flower, L., & Hayes, J.R. (1981). A cognitive process theory of writing. *College Composition and Communication, 32*, 365–387.

> This is one of the first descriptions of Flower and Hayes's cognitive model of writing development. In this work, they describe four key points about writing development as well as their three proposed stages of writing development—pre-write, write, and re-write.

Graham, S., & Harris, K.R. (2003). Students with learning disabilities and the process of writing: A meta-analysis of SRSD studies. In H.L. Swanson, K.R. Harris, & S. Graham (Eds.), *Handbook of learning disabilities* (pp. 323–344). New York: Guilford Press.

Strategic Processing in Academic Domains

This handbook chapter reviews and synthesizes studies using Graham and Harris's Self-Regulatory Strategy Development model. This model is designed to facilitate students' self-regulation, content knowledge, and motivation for writing, with a particular focus on students with disabilities. One of the most salient findings of this meta-analysis relates to the inability of many students with disabilities to access their prior knowledge.

Seven
Mathematical Strategies

Finley is asked to solve a mathematics problem in which she must determine how much fencing she would need to surround a rectangular yard that is 15 feet by 25 feet. First, Finley decides to draw herself a picture of the problem, which represents the yard and where the fence would go. She sees that there are two sets of equal sides and this reminds her of the formula for perimeter, which is P = 2L + 2W. She doubles the length and width, adds them together, and comes up with her answer—80 feet of fencing. She then takes her answer and checks to make sure it makes sense with the drawing she had made previously.

In mathematics, domain-specific strategies were initially focused on mathematics word problems, such as the one Finley was trying to solve in the vignette. George Pólya's *How to Solve It: A New Aspect of Mathematical Method*, published in 1957, was very influential in examining ways in which individuals solved mathematical problems. He suggested that problem solving progressed in four phases: understand the problem, devise a plan, carry out the plan, and look back.[66] Analyzing this plan, there are a number of different types of strategies that were previously discussed in Chapter 2. First, in understanding the problem, one would expect someone to implement surface-level strategies in an attempt to make sense of the information that was presented. In the second phase, devising a plan, one would expect metacognitive and self-regulatory strategies of planning, monitoring, and controlling to be key. In the third phase, carrying out the plan, one again would expect to see more cognitive strategies—either surface level or deep level—or skills (for instance, algorithms, which will be discussed later) to come to an initial solution. Finally, in the last phase, looking back, we would expect the individual to once again engage in metacognitive strategies and cognitive strategies to check their solution.

In addition to this four-step problem-solving process, Pólya described 67 heuristics that could be enacted to help them problem solve in mathematics. **Heuristics** are rules of thumb that are not always the most optimal or efficient ways to solve a problem, but are sufficient. He presented heuristics that can be useful at each of the four phases in his model. For example, during the looking-back phase, one can ask themselves if the result could be used or derived differently. In the vignette, after Finley derived her answer, she looked back at her drawing to see if the answer actually made sense, a common heuristic discussed by Pólya. These heuristics generally fall under the definition of domain-general strategies, because most of the heuristics Pólya described are examples of self-questioning or self-testing. Since the publication of Pólya's work, this framework has been extended for use in multiple academic domains, particularly with regard to analogical problem solving,[67] which is discussed in the science chapter.

While these more general strategic decisions such as guiding, monitoring, and controlling problem solving were most prevalent in the research literature, others argued that as much or more attention should be paid to what Schoenfeld called "tactical decision making"—in other words, strategies that are more related to the specific problem at hand.[68] However, the focus on more general strategic decisions is still a greater focus in the research literature.[41] Contrary to this emphasis, Schoenfeld envisioned mathematics not as a set of facts to memorize (such as times tables), but rather as a way to understand patterns—similar to the goal of scientific inquiry. He argued that both tactical decision making *and* strategic decisions were critical to making meaning in mathematics through patterns.

Two types of domain-specific mathematical strategies at the tactical level can help one make sense of patterns. These are pictorial strategies and symbolic strategies. **Pictorial strategies** are those that rely on visual-spatial properties of drawings or objects to represent mathematical relationships or patterns.[69] These strategies frequently include the manipulation of either physical objects or mental pictures. In the vignette, Finley actually drew out this representation to better help her visualize the problem space. **Symbolic strategies** are those that rely on using symbols or combinations of symbols to represent mathematical relationships or patterns.[70] For example, when Finley decided to use the area formula, she was relying on a symbolic representation of the problem to help her solve it.

PICTORIAL STRATEGIES

Pictorial strategies can be useful to solve or understand a wide variety of mathematical problems including addition, subtraction, fraction comparisons, and finding geometric patterns, just to name a few. For addition, typical strategies used when first learning to add are count-all, count-on, and dot-notation methods. **Count-all** is a strategy whereby the individual counts both addends on each hand to sum the two together. For example, adding the numbers 3 and 5 could be accomplished by putting three fingers up on your left hand, putting five fingers up on your right hand, then counting all the fingers that are up. This is a pictorial strategy, because the child is using a physical object as a manipulative to aid their problem solving. The prime limitation to this strategy is that one is limited to the number of fingers they have. Thus, adding larger numbers becomes problematic with this particular strategy.

The count-on strategy is an extension of the count-all strategy. **Count-on** is a strategy whereby the individual only counts the smaller of the addends—starting from the larger addend, the individual counts the additional contribution of the smaller addend. For example, adding the numbers 11 and 3 could be accomplished by holding three fingers up, starting at 11, and counting the three fingers from 11 to 12 . . . 13 . . . 14. A child could also do this in the inverse as a strategy to help with subtraction. **Counting-back** is a strategy whereby the individual starts with the minuend (the number one is subtracting from), puts up the number of fingers for the subtrahend (the number one is subtracting from the minuend), and counts backwards. For example, if we wanted to subtract the numbers 11 and 3 (11 − 3 = ?), we would hold three fingers up and starting from 11 would count backwards for each finger we were holding up from 11 to 10 . . . 9 . . . 8. As with counting all, both the count-on and count-back strategies are pictorial strategies because a child is manipulating their fingers to help count either forward in the case of addition or backwards in the case of subtraction.

These strategies can also be extended to multiplication using a **number series** strategy.[11] This treats multiplication as a form of repeated addition. For example, to multiply the numbers 3 and 5, you could count by fives three times (using three fingers to keep track of how many fives the child added), 5 . . . 10 . . . 15. If the child was more comfortable counting by threes, they could do that five times (again using their fingers), 3 . . . 6 . . . 9 . . . 12 . . . 15. As with the count-all, count-on, and count-back

Mathematical Strategies 69

strategies, we are limited by the number of manipulatives we have at our disposal (typically our fingers) to make this work. In order for the number series strategies to work, the child needs to be able to count in a series by that number. For example, a child could not multiply the numbers 7 and 8 if they did not know how to count by either sevens or eights. Additionally, a child could use this method to divide simple numbers in a similar way. If a child wanted to divide the number 15 by 3, they could count by threes until they got to 15, using their fingers to track how many threes it took them to get to 15.

Unlike the count-all, count-on, and count-back strategies, the dot-notation method does not use fingers as manipulatives, rather the Arabic numerals themselves are the pictorial manipulatives. The **dot-notation** is a strategy whereby each letter has a corresponding number of points, or dots, that directly correspond with the value of that Arabic number. Below are some examples of adding using this method. In the upper-left example, one could add 9 and 4 by counting the "dots" of each Arabic numeral to count up to 13. This would be akin to the count-all strategy, except instead of using fingers, a child would use the dots assigned to each numeral. In the third example on the middle top, the child could start with 8, then add 7 by counting the dots in that numeral. This would be akin to the count-on strategy, except using dots in the numeral rather than fingers.

$$
\begin{array}{cccc}
& 7 & & 3 \\
9 & 5 & 8 & 5 & 54 \\
+4 & +6 & +7 & +4 & +63 \\
\\
64 & \Box & \Box & 79 \\
52 & 77 & 54 & 68 \\
+32 & +69 & +89 & +57
\end{array}
$$

Figure 7.1 Example of a dot notation mathematics worksheet
From Simon and Hanrahan (2004). Reprinted with permission.

70 Strategic Processing in Academic Domains

In the figure, there are many different ways to represent more complex addition problems using the dot-notation method. Thus, this method extends counting-all, count-on, and count-back to accommodate larger values in both addition and subtraction. While this method has primarily been used for special populations, such as students with learning disabilities, it is less clear if these are effective for typically developing learners.

More common in the research literature with typically developing learners are the use of number-line strategies. **Number-line strategies** use representational manipulatives—which could become a mental manipulative at some point—to demonstrate relationships in the relative size of numbers. Additionally, the ability to use number lines has been shown to improve children's performance on seriation (i.e., understanding the magnitude of objects in relation to one another) and correspondence tasks (i.e., understanding the magnitude of relationships across two different series—such as a series of puppets and a series of cupboards) in mathematics.[71]

There are also effective pictorial strategies for more complex problems than basic arithmetic. One of the more complex topics for children and adolescents is fractions. One common task that appears frequently on the SAT/ACT quantitative portion asks respondents to compare two fractions and tell which one is greater in magnitude (in other words, which is the larger number?). One pictorial strategy to help determine the magnitude of fractions is by visualizing fractions. **Visualizing fractions** is a strategy whereby the individual visualizes (or draws) the amount of the circle or square that the fraction represents. For instance, we might visualize the fraction $\frac{1}{3}$ like this using a rectangle or a circle:

Mathematical Strategies 71

Then one could compare the area of the circle or square represented by that fraction with the area of the circle or square represented by another, such as $\frac{2}{3}$. So they would compare the pictures side by side to determine which is greater.

Like the other pictorial strategies, visualizing fractions is useful for simple fractions, but becomes much more difficult for more complex fractions. Visualizing $\frac{11}{16}$ and $\frac{19}{24}$ to see if one can come up with the fraction of greater magnitude is much more difficult. Even with the pictures designed to be exactly $\frac{11}{16}$ and $\frac{19}{24}$, it is difficult to determine from the pictures which one is larger. More useful strategies for this type of problem are discussed subsequently in the symbolic strategy section.

Finally, pictorial strategies can also be helpful in understanding different geometric shapes. Technology, such as drawing programs, can help an individual rotate shapes to see what would happen if they rotated them in two-dimensional space. For example, one could see what happened if they turned a triangle upside-down. More exciting even is a new tool—virtual reality—which can allow users to rotate geometric shapes in three dimensions to see how the various sides, angles, and radii would interact in three-dimensional space.[72] One of the additional readings recommended at the conclusion of this chapter describes these advances in much more detail.

SYMBOLIC STRATEGIES

While pictorial strategies can be useful for many of the problems discussed previously, as the complexity of the problem increases it is likely that one would have to rely on symbolic strategies to understand these more complex problems. Multiplication would be a good example of an arithmetic function in mathematics, where finger counting is not plausible given the limited number of digits (fingers) one has to work with, or the numbers get large enough that counting in a series is too onerous. A symbolic way to represent this type of more complex problem is through **decomposition**. If the child is asked to multiply the numbers 4 and 6 and cannot directly recall the answer, they may decompose the problem (using the concept of multiplication as repeated addition).[73] This requires that they know some closely related symbolic representation, such as the solution to 4 times 5. They could then simply add one more "4" to that answer to get 24.

As the pictorial strategies discussed previously rely on the inverse relations between addition/subtraction and multiplication/division, symbolic strategies can be used to help children understand this inverse relation. One such strategy is having a child rearrange numbers and symbols in open sentence problems.[74] Presenting the child with the problem: $2 + * = 8$ could be solved by understanding the symbolic relation between the plus and equals operators in that particular problem. In other words, the child could rearrange the problem to read: $8 - 2 = *$. Then, the child could either recall the answer to that subtraction problem or use the counting back strategy. Similarly, one could think of examples in multiplication and division that this strategy would be useful for. The equation $5 \times * = 15$ could be rearranged to read: $15 \div 5 = *$, where the child could again either recall it from memory or use one of the pictorial strategies discussed previously.

Strategies in mathematics are also useful for more subjective tasks (tasks that could have multiple acceptable answers)

Mathematical Strategies 73

than arithmetic, which are more objective tasks (there is typically only one acceptable answer). One of these tasks that is illustrative of some of these strategies is finding the midpoint in a series of numbers. To decide what the midpoint of a series of numbers is, individuals could use what have been termed informal strategies, formal strategies, or both.[75] There are numerous possible informal strategies, so the clumping strategy will be offered as a representative example of this type. The **clumping strategy** is where an individual simply finds the largest "clump" of data that they see, regardless of the other values. Consider a relatively small and simple series of numbers:

Using the clumping strategy, the midpoint here would likely be around seven or eight, because that is where the biggest "clump" of numbers occurs. In this example, seven happens to be the mode (the most repeated value), so the clumping strategy at least would help the person solving this problem arrive at one of the more commonly used values for midpoint. However, this strategy breaks down when there is no mode. For example, if 7, 8, and 9 were the "clump" in the number series (the numbers 7 and 8 were not repeated), there would be no mode but these numbers would still be the closest together in the series, however, this might not be entirely representative of a midpoint for these values.

More formal strategies to evaluate the midpoint would be the use of an estimating heuristic, such as the mean or the median.[75] Not using an algorithm, someone might rely on one of the heuristics Pólya discussed in his earlier work to find the midpoint. These heuristics, such as estimating, however, might lead to a wide variety of solutions to this particular problem of finding the midpoint. One might estimate the midpoint to be somewhere around 15 for those data, and someone else may estimate it a bit higher, say around 20. This is a relatively fast way to describe the midpoint, but there might not necessarily be agreement in these estimating heuristics. These differences would likely be due to the different problem-solving experiences individuals have had in their lives.

To reduce these discrepancies, one could rely on an algorithm, such as the **mean** (the arithmetic average of the values in the series) or the **median** (the midpoint of the values arranged from smallest to largest). Each of these algorithms would each yield a unique solution of 23.5 and 10 respectively for the first set of data shown. However, one would still be left with the decision of whether the mean or median was the better indicator of the midpoint. This may involve another heuristic that Pólya described in determining what the midpoint may be used for.

Finally, when comparing fractions, symbolic strategies can also be used, particularly when the fractions are closer together in value. Consider the following fractions:

$$\frac{11}{23} ? \frac{13}{25}$$

Assume that one is trying to figure out which of these fractions is greater. One could use a number of strategies including noticing the values are on opposite sides of a known reduced fraction and multiplying to obtain common denominators.[76] **Multiplying to obtain common denominators** is the process of multiplying both the numerator (top) and denominator (bottom) of each fraction by a specific value such that one would get the same value in each denominator. Then, one could directly compare each of the numerators directly. For instance, one could simply multiple the numerator and denominator of the fraction on the left by 25 and the numerator and denominator of the fraction on the right by 23 to get a common denominator of 575 for each of the fractions. Multiplying the numerator on the left also by 25 would give us 275, and multiplying the numerator on the right by 23 would give us 299, leaving the following fractions with a common denominator of 575:

$$\frac{275}{575}?\frac{299}{575}$$

Now, one can directly compare the numerators and conclude that the fraction on the left is *smaller* than the fraction on the right.

However, there may be a more efficient strategy in this particular case. Given the computational nature of this problem, solving this with a calculator would take about a minute or so to solve it. However, if this affordance was not available, an opposite-sides approach could be employed. The **opposite-sides** approach involves evaluating each fraction in relation to a given common fraction, such as one-half. Going back to the original fractions,

$$\frac{11}{23}?\frac{13}{25}$$

one could evaluate the left fraction in relation to one-half and the right fraction in relation to one-half. Recalling that 11 is less than half of 23, one could determine that this fraction is *less than* one-half. Likewise, recalling that 13 is more than half of 25, one could determine that it is *more than* one-half. Therefore, the fraction on the right must be larger in magnitude because it is more than one-half and the fraction on the left is less than one-half. This strategy could be extended to other common fractions such as one-third or three-fourths. One drawback to this strategy is that one would not know exactly how much bigger one fraction is than the other (with the common denominator strategy one could know that the fraction on the right is about 4% larger than the one on the left), but if one simply wanted to know which one is bigger, the opposite-sides approach is definitely more efficient and does not require a calculator.

DEVELOPMENT OF STRATEGIES IN MATHEMATICS

While the strategies discussed here only scratch the surface of all the domain-specific strategies in mathematics, hopefully they exemplify how certain strategies may work better (or worse) in certain situations and further how one might expect them to change over time.

With regard to development over time, recall from Chapter 3 that Siegler and Jenkins's Overlapping Waves Theory (OWT) stated that strategies come and go in waves, and, additionally, that children may use multiple strategies at a time. A fairly typical sequence of strategy use would be children starting with the count-all strategy, moving to the count-on strategy, and finally storing and retrieving the answer from long-term memory.[77] Eventually, these strategies could become routinized—particularly the retrieval strategy—so

Mathematical Strategies 77

that it becomes skillful (effortless and unintentional). While being strategic about solving these simple addition problems is good at first, and helps develop an understanding of counting and adding, children become much more efficient and skillful with their addition approaches in order to turn their effort toward more difficult tasks (like fraction magnitude comparisons). There is also likely social desirability at play here—adults would likely not be comfortable counting on their fingers in front of others.

Similar to the shift that occurs in those pictorial strategies, there is also a general shift from pictorial strategies to symbolic strategies.[78] As noted previously, these shifts allow children to handle more complex problems with much larger (and smaller fractional) numbers. This, however, should not be construed to mean that strategies that rely on representational drawing, or creating a mental image of pictorial manipulatives, are no longer useful. Indeed, these may be particularly useful as individuals move toward late competence and expertise and engage in ever more complex learning and problem solving.

In certain circumstances, there are also shifts from more heuristic strategies to domain-specific strategies. A learner's increased conditional knowledge (knowing when and why to apply a certain piece of declarative or procedural knowledge)[79] allows them to choose more specific domain-specific strategies than they would have used in the stage of acclimation. Going back to the example of trying to describe the midpoint of a set of numbers, individuals may move from an estimating heuristic, to using the median or mean, to finally being able to pick the median or the mean depending on the situation at hand. For example, if the data are normally distributed, choosing the mean is customary, while the median is more typical for nonnormally distributed data.

Evidence in the research literature also supports the hypothesis in OWT that multiple strategies may be used at once. First, evidence has shown that using multiple strategies generally produces better learning outcomes, especially at younger ages.[80] However, as children get older they tend to use less multiple strategies, particularly counting-on as a "backup" strategy.[76]

But, as mentioned earlier, for these newer strategies to be successful, individuals must possess more and more cohesive domain knowledge for this progression to occur. For one, lower achievers at the post-secondary level (e.g., community college) still show some differences in strategy use and the efficiency of that strategy use than their higher performing counterparts.[76] One reason for these differences may be the domain knowledge that individuals within each of these groups possesses.

Thus, starting with very complex, domain-specific strategies may not be the optimal path toward good problem solving or domain expertise. Sometimes, the fastest, most efficient strategy does not enable a learner to see the bigger conceptual problem.[81] For example, while retrieval of addition facts from long-term memory is faster and more efficient, skillful or strategic retrieval of knowledge from long-term memory does not help a child understand *what* addition is conceptually. Therefore, they may rely on more general problem solving strategies, starting with simpler pictorial and symbolic strategies, and gradually replace them with more efficient strategies as they learn principles of mathematics.[81]

It is also important to consider that these mathematics strategies, and mathematics knowledge more generally, may be particularly important strategies to possess as expertise is built in a wide variety of academic domains. Learning in academic domains such as physics and engineering that rely heavily on mathematics may hinge on the learner's ability to engage in these mathematical strategies.

ADDITIONAL READINGS

Pólya, G. (1957). *How to solve it: A new aspect of mathematical method.* London: Penguin.

Pólya's book describes heuristics during mathematical problem solving and provides a glossary of 67 heuristics with examples for each. These heuristics can be used during each of the four phases of problem solving: understanding the problem, devising a plan, carrying out the plan, and looking back.

Schoenfeld, A. H. (1983). Episodes and executive decisions in mathematical problem solving. In R. A. Lesh & M. Landau (Eds.), *Acquisitions of mathematics concepts and processes* (pp. 345–395). New York: Academic Press.

Schoenfeld stresses the need for a more domain-specific account of problem solving in mathematics, while retaining much of Pólya's earlier description of mathematical problem solving. Schoenfeld extends Pólya's description by differentiating between tactical and strategic decisions which correspond generally to cognitive and metacognitive strategies in this book. He stresses mathematical strategies as those aimed at finding patterns to describe the world.

Goldman, S. R. (1989). Strategy instruction in mathematics. *Learning Disability Quarterly,* 12, 43–55.

This article discusses particular issues for strategy use in mathematics for children with learning disabilities. The main focus of the article is on instructional techniques to enable children with disabilities to effectively use these strategies. The focus of the instruction is on both cognitive and metacognitive processes.

Geary, D. C., Hoard, M. K., Byrd-Craven, J., & DeSoto, M. C. (2004). Strategy choices in simple and complex addition: Contributions of working memory and counting knowledge for children with mathematical disability. *Journal of Experimental Child Psychology,* 88, 121–151.

This empirical study describes finger counting strategies that are used along a cross-sectional sample of elementary school students from grades one through five with learning disabilities as well as their typically developing peers. The authors contend that the shift to more complex addition problems was possible due to a concurrent shift in mathematics strategy use, which included finger counting.

Eight
Science Strategies

Tiel visits a science museum in her hometown, where she sees an exhibit that describes the changes to the Earth's climate as a result of carbon dioxide emissions in the atmosphere by various man-made and natural sources. She is curious how some of these sources of carbon dioxide affect the Earth, such as sea level rise. At home, she finds a computer simulation program online (such as the C-Learn Simulation).[82] In this simulator, she can adjust multiple variables such as the rate that carbon dioxide is being emitted for both developed and developing countries, the amount of annual reduction in carbon dioxide by these countries, and efforts to prevent deforestation. She starts by manipulating only one of the carbon dioxide emission variables, the annual reduction rate of carbon dioxide emissions for developed countries, and examines how that change affects sea level rise. Then, she resets that variable and chooses another variable to manipulate, the level of deforestation, and sees what effect that has on sea level rise. She continues to tinker with these variables individually until she quickly loses track of how each variable affects sea level rise. She decides that rather than tinkering with each variable individually, she will change a few variables that she thinks will combine to create a specific change in sea level rise—changes in peak carbon dioxide emissions and rates of deforestation. She goes through multiple iterations of this process, specifically targeting the amount of sea level rise that would keep her house in south Florida above sea level.

Learning in science and the strategies used when learning science topics have been primarily situated in studies of text processing[41] or as scientific word problems that rely primarily on mathematics strategies,[83] such as calculating how fast an object falls from a certain height, rather than on scientific experimentation. While the lack of research on domain-specific science strategies is disheartening, it is important to recognize that learning from text and the reading strategies used while reading *about* science are certainly important. For instance, studies have examined what students learn about chemical bonding through text.[84] Particularly for scientific phenomena that can be observed, such as chemical bonding, reading is one of the primary mechanisms by which we learn about science. The same goes for mathematics, particularly because mathematics as described by Schoenfeld[68] and science are both viewed as pattern-finding activities. Thus, it should be no surprise that domain-specific strategies in mathematics will play a predominant role in science learning as well.

One specific example of a mathematics strategy discussed in Chapter 7 that can also apply to science is representational drawing in science. Representational drawing in science can accomplish numerous aims including increasing engagement, representing complex phenomena, scientific reasoning, and communicating with other scientists.[85] For instance, sound waves can be difficult to understand; however, through drawing these sound waves learners may better understand the complex relations between time, air particle movement, and pressure variation.

However, despite the reliance on reading and mathematics strategies for science, it is important to examine the unique strategies that are specific to the physical and life sciences as well, even though there is less empirical study of these. Concept mapping would be a good example of a domain-specific strategy for science that eventually became what could be considered a domain-general strategy as described in Chapter 4. While concept mapping can be useful for a number of different domains and topics (a concept-map about slavery in history, for example), it is a particularly useful technique to uncover some of the patterns that exist in the physical and life sciences. For example, consider the complexities of a biological ecosystem such as a swamp. The complex interrelations in the food chain, habitat, and other interactions between the numerous flora and fauna in that swamp would be difficult (particularly for someone with limited prior knowledge) to conceptualize. A concept map can be a good way to reify those complex relationships. Other domain-specific strategies in science include inquiry-based strategies, spatial strategies, use of schematics, relational reasoning, and epistemic strategies.

INQUIRY-BASED STRATEGIES

Inquiry-based strategies can be used to better understand the patterns of relations between constructs (or concepts in the physical and life sciences). These types of strategies help the learner examine how variables within a scientific model influence each other. Two such examples of these strategies are the control of variables strategy and the history cued strategy. **Control of variables** refers to the strategy of only manipulating one variable at a time in order to see what the effect of that particular variable is on some outcome variable.[86] In the vignette at the beginning of the chapter, Tiel attempts to use this strategy in her manipulation of the individual sources of carbon dioxide. She does this one at a time rather than changing multiple variables at once. This enables her to isolate the effects of that particular variable, for example deforestation, on a particular outcome or outcomes, such as sea level rise. While this control of variables strategy can be effective in identifying the role of individual variables, one drawback to this particular strategy is that learners are not able to take into account the joint effects of the variables—such as interaction effects between the variables.[87]

While isolating variables through the control of variables strategy may be effective for relatively simple two-variable systems, other strategies may help learners understand the more complex effects in three- or more-variable scientific models. One such strategy to help evaluate more complex models is the history cued strategy. The **history cued** strategy is the process of generating and testing hypotheses about the joint effects of multiple variables to see which of these joint effects leads to a certain end state for the outcome variable or variables.[88] In the vignette, after Tiel became frustrated with the amount of time she spent isolating the variables with the control of variables strategy, she turned to a history cued strategy of generating and testing specific hypotheses with a targeted rate of sea level rise. Using this strategy, each of the past findings could contribute to a new, revised hypothesis that is subsequently tested so the findings of each new experiment do not stand in isolation.

SPATIAL STRATEGIES

In addition to using inquiry and experimental strategies to understand relations between constructs, some fields of science rely on spatial strategies, particularly geology. In geology, there have been investigations into how learners observe various geologic features and the strategies they use during these observations. These **field observation strategies** involve examinations and identification of important geologic features such as *strike* and *dip*—the horizontal and vertical planes in geology.[89]

Spatial recognition has also been a component in quite a few investigations into science learning through hypermedia (information presented in multiple modes such as text, graphics, animation, audio, or video in a non-linear way).[90] The different modalities in hypermedia, including being able to animate movement, can also be tools to both display spatial relationships as well as allow students to strategically manipulate spatial relations between objects. For example, a hypermedia environment about pulleys can allow learners to see how pulleys work,[91] and in some cases allow students to simulate how different forces in time and space can change how that pulley works.

USE OF SCHEMATICS

Similar to the use of hypermedia to represent spatial representations, schematics can be used to represent relations, not only spatially, but also graphically. These could be considered types of representational drawings discussed earlier in the chapter. Schematics, like hypermedia, are non-linear and can more easily allow the learner to transform the task or problem.[92] Thus, schematics have the potential to engage learners in deep-level processing if the learner can use them effectively. The issue here is, of course, whether the learner can effectively understand or create a schematic in order to transform the problem.

Below is an example of a fictitious chart that shows some information for a flight from New York to Los Angeles:

Table 8.1 Example table of flight information

Airline	Cost	Flight Time	Type of Plane	Meal Served?
Comfort Airways	$500	4 hrs 45 min	LuxuryJet 440	Yes
On-time Airways	$550	5 hrs 15 min	EconomyJet 175	Yes
Gold-star Airlines	$475	5 hrs 3 min	LuxuryJet 440	Yes
Lucky Duck Airways	$375	6 hrs 10 min	EconomyJet 175	No

The decision which flight to take is relatively complex, because there is a variety of factors at play (e.g., cost, time). In order to effectively make use of all this information, the learner needs to be able to process this information in such a way as to make sense of the problem at the very least in a more surface-level way, or transform the information into something more meaningful for themselves in a deeper-level way. Interestingly, children (and by extension those who have little prior knowledge about what is presented in a schematic) make better associations between the information presented when they examine the attributes rather than the individual cases, or considering both the attributes and the individual cases simultaneously (a unified strategy).[93] Going back to the flights listed in the sample table, it would be better to compare the attributes of each flight (compare all tickets on price) than look at the attributes of the flights individually (flight 1: cost, time, etc. followed by flight 2: cost, time, etc. and so on) or trying to make associations on attributes and flights simultaneously.

RELATIONAL REASONING

Another category of strategies that has been particularly prevalent in scientific domains is relational reasoning. While relational reasoning and spatial reasoning are often considered individual difference variables, the use of that reasoning can be considered strategic if individuals train and use that reasoning in purposeful ways to learn or solve problems in science. As with some of the previous strategies, while these relational reasoning strategies have been used frequently in the physical and life sciences, they also have applicability in other domains as well. Given that relational reasoning is the ability to discern patterns among data or a stream of information,[94] the congruence of these processes, which could be used strategically, with science as a pattern-finding enterprise makes sense. There are four general types of relational reasoning that have been investigated in science that could be used strategically to discern patterns in data—these are analogy, anomaly, antinomy, and antithesis.[95]

Analogy or analogical thinking is a way to understand patterns and relations of data in one area by comparing it to another area that has some structural similarity. Dumas described one such common analogy for electric circuits as water flowing through pipes.[95] This particular analogy works well because each of these systems is a network. Given individuals' familiarity with how water flows through pipes, they can apply this thinking to how electrical circuits work. In fact, analogical reasoning (and the related literature on transfer) has broad potential to act as a bridging mechanism *between* academic domains. Because academic domains are socially constructed, the fluid boundaries between them may be negotiated better by a learner who can see patterns across those domain boundaries, particularly in cases of far transfer (using knowledge from one domain in another unrelated domain).[96] For example, Tiel might use her experiences with the control of variables strategies in the climate problem to a related problem in another domain such as economics. She might use this strategy in a simulation about the effects of free trade agreements on different countries' gross domestic product. This would be an example of far transfer between the physical sciences and economics.

Anomaly is an occurrence in a set of data or information that differs from the overall pattern in those data.[97] For the climate simulation in the vignette, looking for anomalous data in sea level rise might be an effective way to determine if some of the carbon dioxide inputs deviate from the expected or intended relations in the climate model. Looking for anomalous data paired with the history cued strategy could even make a particularly effective strategy combination. **Antinomy** is the process of identifying incompatibilities among concepts—in other words, ruling out possible conclusions or solutions to a problem based on more likely solutions.[98] Again, Tiel could use antinomy as a way to purposefully try to identify which sets of carbon dioxide inputs in which particular sets of developing and developed countries produces differential sea level rise with an eye toward identifying the most likely solution toward acceptable sea level rise. Finally, **antithesis** is the process of observing contrary effects of the same action in two different situations.[99] In Tiel's climate simulation example, she might test whether preventing deforestation in developing countries has a differential effect on sea level rise from that same adjustment in developed countries. She may find that the relation between deforestation in developed countries is antithetical to that of the relation between deforestation in developing countries forming a higher-order relation of opposition between this set of relations.

EPISTEMIC STRATEGIES ABOUT THE NATURE OF SCIENCE

As previously discussed in Chapter 2, there are three levels of strategy use—epistemic, metacognitive, and cognitive. Many of the cognitive strategies in the physical and life sciences previously discussed may only be effective if students also engage in metacognitive strategies (monitoring and controlling cognitive strategies) *and* epistemic strategies that are linked to epistemic beliefs (beliefs about the nature of knowledge and knowing).

In science education, a major focus is the development of students' conceptions of the nature of science (NOS).[100] Two specific epistemic strategies that may be important in this regard are knowledge-based validation and consistency checking. **Knowledge-based validation** is using what they already know to determine if information presented to them is plausible or true.[101] For instance, Tiel might have used what she learned at the science museum about current sea level rise to compare the results of her various manipulations in the climate simulator she used online. **Consistency checking** is determining whether the information presented is congruent with and justified by other information also presented.[101] In this case, Tiel might seek out other models of global climate change to see if the particular relations between carbon dioxide inputs is the same across multiple models of climate change. While these strategies—knowledge-based validation and consistency checking—are presented here as epistemic strategies, these strategies may overlap with metacognitive and self-regulatory strategies. For instance, consistency checking could be a metacognitive strategy used during reading. However, these two strategies are presented here in the science chapter because pattern finding and the use of evidence is a critical part of science teaching and learning.

DEVELOPMENT OF STRATEGIES IN SCIENCE

The strategies discussed in the preceding sections differed from those in the other domains thus far (reading, writing, and mathematics) in that they were at a slightly larger grain size (not specific to certain tasks). Given the many sub-disciplines of the physical and life sciences and the large diversity in tasks within those disciplines, a description of strategy use in science was aimed more at inquiry and reasoning in the sciences, two processes which would also have applicability in other domains (such as history, which is the subject of the next chapter).

In terms of the development of strategy use, particularly for children and adolescents, what might a trajectory of strategy use look like? Here the Model of Domain Learning (MDL) can be most helpful as well as considering the nature of science curriculum during secondary and post-secondary education. First, at the secondary level, adolescents are typically involved in survey-type courses (e.g., introduction to biology), where there are no specific specializations. In other words, there is a focus on the breadth of scientific understanding, rather than depth in one particular specialty or sub-field. For example, adolescents might dissect a number of animals to understand broadly different anatomical features of worms, reptiles, and mammals, but there typically is not in-depth investigation of any one of these animals. In other words, there is little need to have specialized dissection strategies. Rather, learners might rely more on reasoning skills and strategies such as analogic and antithetical reasoning to understand similar and dissimilar skeletal or exoskeletal structures in those animals.

Not until learners start to specialize in a particular field (e.g., virology) would they begin to build very specialized strategies for dealing with problems unique to that specialty area. For example, one would have to have a lot of domain knowledge to understand the processes by which genes can be inserted in the embryo of an organism. However, in order to develop those domain-specific strategies, they would need to build on a base of more general strategies (such as inquiry, spatial, schematic, and reasoning strategies) in order to understand the complexities of problems encountered during the proficiency stage. Thus, as the MDL predicted, one would expect to see shifts from the use of very domain-general, surface-level strategies as children solving science problems and tasks to very domain-specific, deep-level creation of new problems and new knowledge as experts in their field.

ADDITIONAL READINGS

Novak, J.D. (1990). Concept mapping: A useful tool for science education. *Journal of Research in Science Teaching*, 27, 937–949.

> Unlike the concept map article suggested in Chapter 4, this article discusses the use of concept mapping specifically in science, the first academic domain where it saw widespread use. It describes the history of concept mapping in science and discusses the particular uses of concept mapping to evaluate long-term changes in students' knowledge representation of complex science topics.

Dumas, D. (2016). Relational reasoning in science, medicine, and engineering. *Educational Psychology Review*, 1–23. doi:10.1007/s10648-016-9370-6

> This review examines how relational reasoning is used in the physical and life sciences as well as medicine and engineering. It provides examples of each of the four different types of relational reasoning—analogy, anomaly, antinomy, and antithesis—and gives examples for each from the research literature. Additionally, the review discusses ways in which these reasoning processes have been investigated.

Hmelo-Silver, C.E., & Azevedo, R. (2006). Understanding complex systems: Some core challenges. *Journal of the Learning Sciences, 15*, 53–61.

In this article, the authors discuss particular issues that arise when dealing with complex systems. Notions of these complex systems being viewed as either emergent or causal are explored using a biology topic—the human circulatory system—as a complex topic in which to exemplify some of the issues related to understanding these complex systems.

Nine
Social Studies Strategies

Liz's ninth grade history assignment is to examine the causes and outcomes of the American and French Revolutions. She decides to create a list of the causes and outcomes of each revolution, making a list of similarities and differences between each. She examines primary source documents by George Washington, Thomas Jefferson, Marquis de Lafayette, and Napoleon Bonaparte. She listed some similarities of the grievances these writers had about the current governments of the American colonies and France, respectively. One issue that was common across both revolutions was that each revolutionary group believed the system of taxation was unfair. However, one key difference was that the Americans sought to overthrow British authorities and become an independent nation, whereas the French sought to overthrow their own ruling monarchy.

Like the science strategies discussed in the previous chapter, most of the strategies discussed in the research literature for social studies tend to be somewhere between domain-general and domain-specific strategies, meaning that these strategies may encompass multiple domains. In the physical and life sciences, there was quite a bit of overlap between science and mathematics, whereas in the social studies literature there tends to be greater overlap with reading and writing because these are major tools in the domain, particularly with regard to history. Three specific areas of social studies have received more attention in the literature with regard to

Social Studies Strategies 93

domain-specific strategies: historical inquiry, geography, and government and politics.

HISTORICAL INQUIRY

Similar to science, those engaged in historical inquiry have also placed emphasis not only on cognitive strategy use, but also on the epistemic strategies necessary to carry out those cognitive strategies. At the broadest level, strategic decompositions such as **compare and contrast** can be used to help learners begin to analyze historical artifacts.[102] For example, in the vignette Liz identified one comparison between the revolutions (taxation as a root cause) and one major contrast (creation of an independent nation versus changing a nation's system of government). In other words, the tools of historical inquiry (and by extension the strategic processing that takes place during that inquiry) require strategies that provide new insights over and above learners' naïve (or untrained) thinking about history, which requires a reframing about how one thinks and strategizes during the historical inquiry process.[103]

One of the most critical aspects of historical inquiry is source work. **Source work** involves four cognitive acts—identification, attribution, perspective judgment, and reliability assessment.[104] Identification is the process of knowing what the source is. For example, Liz had to identify who had written each of the primary sources she read—Washington, Jefferson, de Lafayette, and Bonaparte. Attribution is knowing that the author of the source created an artifact for a particular purpose. Judging perspective means studying what the source said in relation to the relevant context, which includes time, place, and competing accounts of what happened. For example, Liz might want to look at other primary sources, such as that of King George III. Finally, reliability assessment involves comparing one account from an artifact to other accounts in other artifacts to corroborate the underlying events. Thus, Liz might examine King George III's account and Jefferson's account to see which events could be corroborated.

Many of these source processes just discussed have been gaining more attention in the research literature, particularly in light of the way in which sources and artifacts are available through the internet.[105] These have included studies of multiple texts,[106] multiple search results,[107] and the computer environments[108] in which the sources are housed. Additionally, most of the research on this type of sourcework has occurred in the context of historical artifacts that are textual. Therefore, not only are the strategies related to sourcework necessary to engage in historical inquiry, the historian must also possess critical literacy.[104]

Critical literacy is the act of interrogating multiple viewpoints.[109] Therefore, with this heavy emphasis on reading and comprehending written text, it is no surprise that domain-specific strategies of reading will also play a large role in historical inquiry. For example, in order to interrogate different points of view, reading strategies aimed at understanding the argument are acute. Strategies such as questioning and global restatements of the argument would also be core to engaging in source work.

GEOGRAPHY

Similar processes to historical inquiry have been proposed when learning about geography. Specific strategies have been suggested that map onto the main principles in geography such as *cause and effect, classification, systems,* and *locations.*[110] For example, creating and using maps can help learners rely on visual cues and sketching to situate multiple geographic features in context. Sketching the elevations of two places—such as Iowa versus Colorado—can allow the learner to visualize different topographies and the economic systems that might be in place there. In this example, the topography of Iowa would lend itself to farming more so than Colorado. Other features could be sketched and mapped to further enhance one's understanding.

Another strategy discussed in the literature is that of photo documentation. **Self-directed photo documentation** enables learners to use photographic evidence in order to interpret similar and different events from multiple perspectives.[111] For example, students could be given cameras and asked to create image-based projects, as Ali-Khan and Siry did with children from Pakistan and Luxembourg to envision their multiple perspectives on the knowledge economy.[112]

GOVERNMENT AND POLITICS

Finally, in government and politics there has been a focus on social interaction strategies to understand domain processes. Three such strategies include simulations such as Model UN and Mock Trial. **Simulations** are learning environments in which the features of a typical domain problem are structured in such a way as to enable learners to extract key features of that problem. One such structured simulation in government and politics is Model UN. Model UN simulations can give students the opportunity to engage in negotiation strategies, argumentation strategies, and consensus building strategies.[113] Similarly, Mock Trial can also create a simulation framework that encourages strategy use. Argumentation strategies, dealing with epistemic ambiguity, and writing legal briefs are three such strategies facilitated during Mock Trial.[114]

DEVELOPMENT OF STRATEGIES IN SOCIAL STUDIES

Similar to science, the development of strategies in social studies relies on learners having a cohesive base of both domain-general strategies as well as domain-specific strategies in reading and writing. This reliance on principled knowledge relates particularly to inquiry in history, although this would be relevant for the other areas of social studies discussed here as well. VanSledright described the changes in historical thinking (and the strategies associated with it) along a trajectory similar to that of the Model of Domain Learning (MDL) described.[104] Another useful framework that paralleled VanSledright's description of historical thinking is Wineburg's framework of historical problem solving.[115]

According to VanSledright, learners initially would engage in historical inquiry with few to no strategies. They might see history as either given (there is only one unique possible view of history) or inaccessible (that it is impossible to have any unique view of history). Here, there is no reason to engage in any strategic thinking because there is no problem (similar to absence of critical thinking from an epistemic perspective when the objective or subjective dominates).[116] Gradually, as children move into adolescence and begin to build a base of domain-general and domain-specific strategies in domains such as reading and writing, they become intelligent novices—relying on domain-general strategies to understand problems in history.[104] For example, a sixth grader may not engage in a reliability assessment to corroborate sources, as an expert historian would, but if they have developed domain-specific deep-level strategies in reading—like making a global restatement about the argument—they begin to lay the groundwork for that later sourcework.

As learners engage in sourcework, either through document search or simulations, it becomes necessary for that learner to understand context and point of view in order to interpret a historical event or engage in a negotiation as part of a Model UN simulation. The realization that bias and partisanship can muddy the water, so to speak, induces learners to engage in more strategies if they have also engaged in epistemic and metacognitive strategies.

ADDITIONAL READINGS

VanSledright, B. (2004). What does it mean to think historically . . . and how do you teach it. *Social Education, 68,* 230–233.

> This article lays out a framework for historical inquiry and the processes involved with that historical inquiry. The focus of the article is on sourcework, what it means to think historically, and teaching historical thinking. In particular, the article advocates rethinking history education to facilitate the deep-level processes such as sourcework that are not typically present in history education.

Wineburg, S.S. (1991). Historical problem solving: A study of the cognitive processes used in the evaluation of documentary and pictorial evidence. *Journal of Educational Psychology, 83,* 73–87.

> This article describes ways in which history teachers can help students use primary and secondary sources in their classroom. Using a think-aloud protocol, Wineburg describes the pictorial strategies students used while engaging in historical inquiry using these primary and secondary sources.

Bråten, I., Britt, M.A., Strømsø, H.I., & Rouet, J.F. (2011). The role of epistemic beliefs in the comprehension of multiple expository texts: Toward an integrated model. *Educational Psychologist, 46,* 48–70.

> This review article argues that the integration of multiple sources is key to competent reading. They lay out a model of comprehending multiple texts that includes other factors such as epistemic beliefs.

Part III
Nurturing Strategic Processing

Ten
Influences on Strategy Use

As discussed in the development of domain-specific strategy use in the preceding chapters, strategies do not develop on their own. What, then, influences the development of these strategies? Based on theoretical models previously described, the influences of prior knowledge, interest, broader notions of motivation, epistemic beliefs, and academic emotions will be discussed in this chapter.

PRIOR KNOWLEDGE

As discussed in Chapter 3, the Model of Domain Learning (MDL) described a concurrent rise in **domain and topic knowledge** along with domain-specific, deep-level strategies.[14] These concomitant changes have been reported in multiple domains from special education[15] to kinesthetic tasks such as volleyball.[117] Without both breadth and depth of domain knowledge, it would be very difficult to use domain-specific strategies. For example, thinking back to the titration instance in Chapter 2, there is undoubtedly much declarative knowledge that would need to be retrieved in order to titrate effectively to determine the alkalinity or acidity of a particular solution, such as appropriate titrants to use.

While it is important to understand how the presence or absence of prior knowledge influences strategy use, it is also important to examine how strategy use can build stores of domain and topic knowledge. For instance, the use of reading strategies while reading a complex text can better help someone learn from text, whereas someone reading a complex text without using any strategies is not likely to build an enduring understanding of that text, particularly if they did not engage in any deep-level strategies.[47] Thus, the relation between prior knowledge and strategy use is bidirectional.

INTEREST

The MDL also described links between individual and situational interest and strategic processing. The strongest link between interest and strategic processing is the relation between **individual interest** (i.e., sustained interest in a topic or domain)[16] and strategic processing. For example, Alexander and colleagues reported significant concurrent increases in both individual interest about special education and an increase in the frequency of strategy use in their study.[7] That study—which also showed concurrent increases in domain knowledge—is a good example of how strategic processing can be positioned in terms of both knowledge and interest. Alexander described strategic processing as a "natural link between knowledge and interest."[14] In other words, interest tends to be the precursor to the quantity and quality of strategic processing, while this use of strategic processing in turn builds domain and topic knowledge.

Individual interest is not the only form of interest that may influence strategic processing. **Situational interest** (i.e., externally triggered, task-specific interest)[16] may also influence strategic processing, albeit not always in positive ways. For learners in acclimation and the early stages of competence who have not developed individual interest in the domain, situational interest may be necessary to induce strategy use.[18] For example, in a volleyball task situational interest was positively related to increases in strategic processing.[118] However, there are times when situational interest has negative effects on the usefulness and conditionality of strategic processing. When Garner and colleagues introduced what they coined "seductive details," strategic processing to understand both the main ideas and supporting details of the text negatively influenced performance.[50]

MOTIVATION

While the relation between strategic processing and interest has garnered attention in the research literature because of the MDL, other motivational processes have also been reported to influence strategic processing. One such construct is the motivational goals that students set for themselves. In general, students that set out to learn about the content from a particular task[119] (i.e., mastery goals) use more strategies than those who just seek to do well on that particular task[120] (i.e., performance goals).

While achievement goal theory is not as influential as it once was, other theoretical models, such as self-determination theory (SDT)[121] can also help shed light on the relation between motivation and strategic processing. In SDT, motivation is considered multidimensional (much like the MDL where domain learning is multidimensional). Not only does the quantity of motivation matter, the quality of that motivation matters as well. Deci and Ryan distinguish between autonomous and controlled motivation. **Autonomous motivation** refers to either intrinsic motivation (interest in learning that particular task or enjoyment of that task) or internalized extrinsic motivation (the learning or task relates to some personal goal, (i.e., relevance). **Controlled motivation**, on the other hand, refers to either external regulation (learning or studying to get a reward or avoid a punishment) or introjected regulation (internalizing external regulation to feel guilt, shame, or anxiety).

Autonomous motivation typically produces better outcomes, chief among them higher grades.[122] However, more germane to the topic at hand, autonomous motivation is related to increased levels of deep processing.[123] This parallels the suggestions of the MDL, that increased individual interest should lead to greater deep-level processing. On the other hand, higher quantities of controlled motivation lead to greater levels of surface processing. Indeed, both clusters of students with good *quality* of motivation (autonomous over controlled) do just as well as those with high *quantity* of motivation (either autonomous or controlled) on the depth of their processing over those that have either low quality or quantity of motivation.[124]

More fine-grained than the motivational regulation one has to engage in a particular task, instrumental goals have also demonstrated a relation to strategic processing. Fryer, Ginns, and Walker contended that goals are central to the pursuit of a strategy stating that, "Goals are fundamental to the planning and pursuit of any strategy."[125] **Instrumental goals** refer to either intrinsic goals (goals that students have control over) and extrinsic goals (external sources that determine said goals). Not only have these goals been shown to influence strategic processing in similar ways as the larger-grained autonomous and controlled motivation,[126] but the nature of individuals' instrumental goals has long-term effects on that processing as well. Instrumental goals that individuals initially possess have been shown to have a large influence on the level of strategic processing 15 months later.[125] Specifically, goals that were internally regulated, such as increasing life opportunities, were strongly positively related to deeper-level processing, while externally related goals, such as making a higher salary, were strongly negatively related to deeper-level processing.

Taken together, these motivational components help explain differences in strategic processing. They suggest that focusing on internal regulation and the development of goals around that internal regulation can have profound effects on individuals' cognitive processing.

EPISTEMIC BELIEFS

The relation between epistemic beliefs and strategic processing is also a burgeoning topic in the educational psychology literature following a few high-profile works in the last decade.[127] While epistemic beliefs (i.e., one's beliefs about the nature of knowledge and knowing) are not likely to impact cognitive strategy use directly, there is new theoretical and empirical evidence that supports such a connection that is mediated by self-regulatory processing. This is similar to how motivational variables discussed previously influence performance, through cognitive variables with strategic processing being one such variable. Muis has described a model in which epistemic beliefs influence goal standards for a given task and these in turn will influence which cognitive strategies to employ.[127] In other words, epistemic beliefs help color individuals' perceptions about a particular task thereby influencing one's strategy choices.

For example, if a learner believes knowledge is objective (i.e., there is only one correct position), a reader engaged in an argumentative text about the existence of extraterrestrial civilizations may be more likely to employ surface-level strategies because they may not be aware of the argumentative nature of the text at all. On the other hand, a learner that believes knowledge is subjective and needs to be justified will likely engage in more deep-level processes because they are likely to try to identify the argument, evidence to support the argument, and evaluate their level of agreement with the text (such as arguing with the text). While the empirical research in this area is still relatively recent, the importance of better understanding these complex relations may be particularly important in computer-based learning environments.[128]

ACADEMIC EMOTIONS

An influence on strategic processing that is also relatively recent is the influence of academic emotions on strategic processing.[129] Pekrun and colleagues' Cognitive-Motivational Model on the Effects of Emotions described the influence that positive and negative emotions can have on other cognitive and motivational variables. They described four types of emotions: **positive activating emotions**, such as enjoyment of learning or pride that *increase* cognitive and motivational mechanisms; **positive deactivating emotions**, such as relief or contentment that *decrease* cognitive and motivational mechanisms; **negative activating emotions**, such as anger or anxiety that *increase* cognitive and motivational mechanisms; and **negative deactivating emotions**, such as boredom or hopelessness that *decrease* cognitive and motivational mechanisms.[130] Thus, with regard to frequency of strategy use, there would be a general prediction that positive and negative activating emotions could both increase strategic processing. For example, a learner that enjoyed engaging in a task like reading about sharks would be more likely to use more strategies than a learner who felt contented. Similarly, an anxious learner would be expected to use more strategies than a learner that was bored.

However, while both positive and negative emotions can be activating in terms of frequency of strategy use, the strategies employed by those feeling such emotions can differ. Negative affect, such as anxiety, has been negatively associated with deep-level strategies.[131] Positive emotions, on the other hand, are more likely to support both deep-level strategies as well as self-regulation.[132]

ADDITIONAL READINGS

Vansteenkiste, M., Sierens, E., Soenens, B., Luyckx, K., & Lens, W. (2009). Motivational profiles from a self-determination perspective: The quality of motivation matters. *Journal of Educational Psychology*, 101, 671–688.

This article describes both the quality and quantity of autonomous and controlled motivation on multiple learning outcomes. Chief among these outcomes is the level of processing that individuals who have those types of motivation typically engage in. This article is also a good example of a person-centered approach to studying these phenomena.

Muis, K.R. (2007). The role of epistemic beliefs in self-regulated learning. *Educational Psychologist*, 42, 173–190.

In this article, Muis describes a theoretical model that articulates the connections between epistemic beliefs and self-regulated learning (in which cognitive strategies would be a component of self-regulated learning). She posits four such propositions about this relation including both affective and cognitive components in this relation, how epistemic beliefs set standards for the learner, and influences that self-regulated learning may have on epistemic beliefs.

Pekrun, R., Goetz, T., Titz, W., & Perry, R.P. (2002). Academic emotions in students' self-regulated learning and achievement: A program of qualitative and quantitative research. *Educational Psychologist*, 37, 91–105.

This article describes a theoretical model based on five previous qualitative studies of academic emotions. Germane to strategic processing, the article discusses how academic emotions are specifically related to strategic processing in terms of both the frequency and type of strategies that learners may employ based on the emotions they identified.

Eleven
Measuring and Evaluating Strategy Use

Before ways to nurture strategies are discussed, it is important to understand what strategies learners may already be using, if a given intervention had an impact, and if those strategies are being used well. In order to understand these three aspects, accurate and consistent ways to measure current and future strategy use have to be considered. This chapter is divided into three subsections: what aspects of strategy use are important to measure, measurements that have been used to quantify and qualify strategy use, and how these measurements can be useful in formative evaluation.

IMPORTANT ASPECTS OF STRATEGY USE TO MEASURE

Dinsmore recently described three aspects of strategy use that have been measured—frequency, usefulness, and conditionality.[41] The most common aspect of strategy use in the contemporary literature has been **frequency**, which is how often (or if at all) strategies have been employed. While it certainly makes intuitive and theoretical sense to measure the frequency of strategy use—as one would expect that the more one engages strategically, the better their performance would be—frequency in and of itself does not consistently relate to performance outcomes in the literature. In other words, there are quite a few studies where frequency of strategy use relates very strongly to performance (i.e., those who engage in a high frequency of strategy use typically have *higher* levels of performance),[133] but also quite a few studies where there is no relation between frequency of strategy use and performance.[134] There are even a few studies where there is an inverse relation between frequency and performance (i.e., those that engage in a high frequency of strategy use typically have *lower* levels of performance).[135] In order for theoretical models to be helpful in a generalizable way, these relations should be consistent across situations.

Possible explanations for these inconsistencies can be found both in Overlapping Waves Theory (OWT) and the Model of Domain Learning (MDL) that were discussed in detail in Chapter 3. Recall that in OWT strategies should become more adaptive over time and that some strategies will disappear[10] (either the individual will stop using them or they will become skillful). Thus, there is an onus on the individual to use the most appropriate strategy in a given situation, which is called **conditionality**. Further, recall in the MDL that certain types of strategies are used more often at different levels of expertise. In acclimation, there is the expectation that individuals are primarily engaging in a greater number of domain-general, surface-level strategies,[18] whereas in proficiency, there is the expectation that individuals are primarily engaged in a greater number of domain-specific, deep-level strategies. If an acclimating learner attempts to use a complex domain-specific, deep-level strategy that they cannot employ well, this strategy is likely to have little to no effect and could possibly make performance worse by expending effort on a useless process.

Thus, measuring the **usefulness** of a strategy is also important to understanding whether that strategy is ultimately helpful in problem or task completion. The usefulness of a strategy refers to how well a particular strategy works in terms of making progress on a particular problem or task. If the employed strategy does not assist the learner in making progress on a particular task, it is not a useful strategy. For instance, when a reader who does not understand a text passage decides to reread the text, that rereading strategy may or may not be useful. If rereading helps the reader understand that portion of text it is indeed useful; if there is no progress in understanding that text it is not useful. There may be little difference between readers who employ very few strategies (low frequency) and those who employ a lot of strategies, few of which are useful. Simply examining the frequency of strategy use in this case may lead one to conclude that the reader who employs more strategies will comprehend the text better, whereas examining the usefulness of those strategies will tell a more complete story about an individual's strategic processing and performance. Indeed, when usefulness *and* conditionality are taken into account, the relations between strategic processing and performance are much more consistent.[41]

MEASUREMENTS OF STRATEGY USE

Measurements of strategic processing can be divided into three main types—retrospective self-report, concurrent self-report, and observations of observable behavior.[41] Because strategic processing is by definition a covert behavior (i.e., one could not directly observe a cognitive strategy being employed), measurement of strategic processing must be made observable. The effects of those strategic decisions can be observed, and one could then infer that some sort of strategic processing took place, or individuals can be asked to make their covert processing overt (i.e., observable), thereby inferring that these overt reports are accurate representations of their covert strategy use.

Measuring strategic processing by inducing individuals to make their otherwise covert cognitive processing overt through the use of self-report can be further divided into concurrent and retrospective self-report. **Retrospective self-report** measurements ask individuals to overtly state what they have done during a previous problem, task, or experience. This retrospective reporting can take many forms including checklists, Likert-type scales, slider scales, and semi-structured or structured interviews. Strategy checklists typically list a set of possible strategies and ask students to place a checkmark beside any of the listed strategies that they used. This measurement enables the researcher to get a binary measure of whether or not a strategy was used. For example, there might be a list of reading strategies—rereading, underlining, arguing with text as examples—and the participant will be asked to check any that they used. Some similar measures that also use these types of measures can also be **prospective self-report**. Instead of asking what strategies were employed after a task, these measures might ask what strategies an individual may employ during an upcoming or typical task. This approach may be more typical using a theoretical framework that is more trait based than state based.

Alexander and Murphy used a variant of this checklist by additionally having individuals place an asterisk by any strategy that they found particularly helpful.[136] Likert-type and slider scale measures extend these binary measurements to enable a continuous measure of frequency. For example, one could take that same list of strategies in the previous example and ask whether a particular strategy was used more frequently or less frequently. While the checklist, Likert-type, and slider scales measure the frequency of strategy use, it is difficult to measure the other aspects of strategic processing

112 Nurturing Strategic Processing

(i.e., usefulness and conditionality) through these methods. One way to measure usefulness from the individual's perspective is to use the method employed by Alexander and Murphy that involves putting an asterisk by those strategies that are deemed particularly helpful.

However, structured and semi-structured interviews may be better suited to measuring the aspects of usefulness and conditionality, at least from the standpoint of the person employing those strategies. **Structured interviews** are measures where there is a standard set of open-ended questions asked of each participant, and they typically respond verbally (however, it could be written). **Semi-structured interviews** are measures where there is an initial set of open-ended questions asked of each participant, but these questions can be modified by the interviewer depending on a participant's previous answer. These interview measurements are the most common ways to further probe the aspects of conditionality and usefulness of strategies from the interviewee's perspective.[41] A variant of these interview approaches is the microanalytic approach, which is a structured interview that examines moment-to-moment questioning that targets cognitive or affective processes.[137]

One of the potential issues with retrospective self-report is whether individuals have the capacity to accurately remember what strategies they employed after a problem or task.[138] Another form of self-report that mitigates this particular issue is the use of concurrent, rather than retrospective, self-report. In the strategic processing literature, the most common form of concurrent self-report is the use of verbal protocol analysis, or the think-aloud protocol (TAP).[41] During TAP, participants are asked to verbalize what they are thinking and doing while they are engaged in a task.[139] These verbal protocols can then be coded for any number of behaviors, including those that are strategic.[140,53] Thus, unlike retrospective self-report, TAP does not rely on memory processes to accurately report strategy use because they are reporting in real time. Concurrent self-reports are not immune to criticism, either. There has been debate about whether interrupting individuals' ongoing processes changes that processing, however, there is little evidence to conclude that it influences cognitive and metacognitive processing.[138] Because these verbalizations can be placed in the context of the problem and task, coders can assess the conditionality and usefulness of those strategies, at least from the coders' perspective.[46]

One additional common issue that has been raised about both these forms of self-report is whether individuals can accurately report their own strategic processing at all.[141] In other words, can inducing these self-reports change the nature of those self-reports? In order to accurately report which cognitive strategies an individual is using, that individual must be able to accurately monitor what they are doing, an issue that is exacerbated when individuals are asked to report on their metacognitive strategy use.[142] This issue is quite complex and controversial in the literature, thus cannot be covered in adequate depth here. For readers interested in more information about this issue, the Veenman, Van Hout-Wolters, and Afflerbach article in the Additional Readings section would be a good starting point for further exploration.

In order to circumvent these issues, some researchers have chosen to examine the effects of that strategic processing, or **observations** of behavior only. These observations can be physical manifestations in the environment such as actions taken during a simulation or electronic traces in computer-based environments (computer log files).[108] Using these observations, inferences are made from the observable behavior (i.e., trace data) to what the covert processing was. This is analogous to studying gravity in physics. One cannot actually observe gravitational forces or gravitational particles, although they are theorized to exist. Rather, the *effects* of those gravitational forces can be directly observed (i.e., an object such as an apple falling from a tree to the ground) and the cause of that effect, gravity, is inferred. The issue here, of course, is that the inferences of the researcher (or whomever is doing the measuring) could be faulty.

Each of these particular measurements has strengths and weaknesses. One suggestion to better ensure that measurements of strategic processing are accurate and consistent is to use multiple approaches. For example, De Backer and colleagues used both concurrent and retrospective self-report in their study of strategy use during peer discussions.[143] Additionally, these multiple approaches can enable the capture of multiple aspects of strategy use—frequency, usefulness, and conditionality—that can better guide teachers' scaffolding of strategy use, a topic addressed in detail in the next chapter.

MEASUREMENTS OF STRATEGY USE AS FORMATIVE EVALUATION

Before turning to instructional strategies that can be used to foster strategic processing, it is necessary to contextualize *when* and *how* measurements of strategic processing may be used by a teacher or more knowledgeable other in a learning situation. First, it is useful to distinguish between two types of assessment—formative and summative. **Formative assessment** is when these data are used to drive instructional or curricular decisions, while **summative assessment** is when these data are used to describe a student's achievement.[144] The focus here will be on the use of formative assessment for strategic processing, as this type of assessment can best guide an exploration of interventions that can be used to assist learners in being more strategic.

Formative assessment is critical for two reasons. First, without knowing what a learner is already doing with regard to strategic processing, it is difficult to design an effective intervention to improve that processing. For example, if a learner is doing poorly at a certain task, like reading an informational text about sharks, designing an intervention aimed at helping them be more strategic would depend on what they were already doing. Imagine one learner, Max, who employs a lot of strategies that are not particularly useful. An intervention to increase his use of strategies would not be likely to help Max improve his performance. Rather, facilitating his metacognitive strategy use and monitoring would be more helpful. Contrast this with Sally, who uses very few strategies, but those that she does use she uses well. In this case, teaching her additional strategies would be more likely to improve performance.

Second, one needs to be able to detect changes or growth in strategic processing to evaluate whether a given intervention was successful for that student or group of students. Utilizing these measurements in the course of a pretest-posttest design (i.e., measuring aspects of strategic processing before and after the intervention) will not only help evaluate the current intervention—did it work or not—but also act as a catalyst for future instruction.

ADDITIONAL READINGS

Dinsmore, D.L. (2017). Towards a dynamic, multidimensional model of strategic processing. *Educational Psychology Review*, 29, 235–268. doi: 10.1007/s10648-017-9407-5.

The review examines strategic processing and the relation between strategic processing by examining three facets of strategy use: frequency, usefulness, and conditionality. Methods of measurement are discussed with regard to how the particular facets of strategy use can be most efficiently examined.

Ericsson, K.A., & Simon, H.A. (1998). How to study thinking in everyday life: Contrasting think-aloud protocols with descriptions and explanations of thinking. Mind, Culture, and Activity, 5, 178–186.

This article discusses think-aloud protocols. As part of a larger special issue, the article specifically addresses some of the criticisms of think-aloud protocols and evidence that supports their use, as well as the theoretical model put forth by Ericsson and Simon.

Pressley, M., & Afflerbach, P. (1995). Verbal protocols of reading: The nature of constructively responsive reading. New York: Routledge.

Pressley and Afflerbach's influential book describes the use of think-aloud protocols specifically with reading. They describe typical reading behaviors and the processes by which one can examine these behaviors by asking individuals to say out loud what they are thinking and doing as they are reading. This is an excellent resource not only for learning how to implement a think-aloud protocol, but is also a good resource for reading behaviors that could be either skillful or strategic depending on how the reader used them.

Bråten, I., & Samuelstuen, M.S. (2007). Measuring strategic processing: comparing task-specific self-reports to traces. Metacognition and Learning, 2, 1–20.

This article is a good example of multiple methods of measuring strategic processing. These authors measured processing by using both self-report and trace methodologies. Additionally, they discussed how these different measurements of strategy use related to performance, with the trace data being more predictive of performance.

Veenman, M.V., Van Hout-Wolters, B.H., & Afflerbach, P. (2006). Metacognition and learning: Conceptual and methodological considerations. Metacognition and Learning, 1, 3–14.

This article synthesizes some of the issues with measuring covert strategy use with an emphasis on the role of metacognitive strategies. This article also offers suggestions for measuring these covert activities for future research.

Twelve

Instructional Principles to Enhance Strategy Use

One of the issues in strategy training research is that there are few studies that focus on domain-specific strategy training appropriate to complete a specific task,[41] but many that focus on general study strategies[21] or metacognitive strategy training.[142] This is not to say that general study and metacognitive strategy training are not important, because particularly at the earlier stages of expertise development in an academic domain these strategies are critical.[18] Indeed, Pintrich discussed at length the need for *both* cognitive and metacognitive strategy training in order for either to be effective.[145] Without the monitoring and control strategies, it would be unlikely that knowing a strategy would be helpful if the learner did not know *how* to use it (i.e., usefulness) or *when* to use it (i.e., conditionality).

Additionally, the need for strategy training and the specific type of strategy training necessary will likely evolve over the course of the learner's development in an academic domain. In the acclimation stages, training for domain-general and metacognitive strategies can be particularly helpful. However, as those learners move toward competence—and particularly proficiency—training for domain-specific strategies becomes crucial.[14] Without these domain-specific strategies, it would be unlikely that a learner could complete the complex tasks that experts are expected to engage in. Domain-general and metacognitive strategy training without domain-specific strategy training would be akin to putting a large down payment on a house without making any of the subsequent mortgage payments. A large down payment (use of effective domain-general and metacognitive strategies) gets one much closer to owning the house, but without making the resulting mortgage payments (use of effective domain-specific strategies), one will not own that house for long.

While the focus of the book is on cognitive strategies, training programs for strategy use have typically encompassed multiple kinds of strategy use, as discussed previously, and multiple instructional methods to teach those strategies. Presented here are five specific instructional approaches to enhance learners' strategy use from the cognitive and metacognitive literature—modeling, prompting and cueing, motivating strategy use, making strategy use meaningful and embedding that strategy use, and focusing on a few strategies at a time. Finally, the chapter will conclude with three principles of strategy instruction suggested by Harris and Pressley.

MODELING

The first approach is a particular instructional strategy that has a long history in the educational psychology literature more generally: modeling. Modeling has its roots in various prominent theories and models of learning including social constructivism,[146] social-cognitive theory,[147] and apprenticeship models.[148] Modeling has also been used extensively with strategy training and has been shown to be particularly effective in a wide variety of domains including reading[149] and computer-based learning environments.[150] Typically, modeling has occurred via a human model, such as a teacher,

Instructional Principles 119

but continued work on the development of intelligent tutoring systems—such as iSTART—can model strategy use for students as well.[151]

The use of modeling as a strategy training technique has been most prevalent for two specific populations. There have been many investigations in strategy training for individuals with disabilities (typically cognitive disabilities) in the domains of mathematics[152] and writing.[58] Additionally, there is a robust literature base that has investigated the use of modeling to train strategies for English language learners (ELLs).[153] While some of these strategy trainings used special populations such as students with disabilities and ELLs, there is no reason these modeling techniques would not be helpful for typically developing students as well.

Two such examples of modeling strategy use in the classroom are using think-alouds in reading and the count-on strategy in mathematics. First, with regard to reading, as the teacher reads aloud, that teacher could also say out loud any strategies they might be using as they are reading to comprehend the text. For example, after reading a particular sentence about ocean life, the teacher could say, "That sentence reminded me about a time I went to the beach and saw dolphins swimming close to the shoreline." This would model the strategy of connecting to personal experience (discussed in more detail in Chapter 5) that if used by students could encourage deep-level processing. This modeling is often done as students enter the classroom to get them seated quietly or could be used as students read aloud. Modeling would also be a good instructional approach for manipulative strategies such as the count-on strategy in mathematics (discussed in more detail in Chapter 7). Rather than explaining the strategy, simply demonstrating its use with a few addition problems might be more effective, particularly for younger learners for whom this strategy is particularly appropriate. Pictorial strategies in mathematics would be particularly good candidates for this modeling approach as well.

PROMPTING AND CUEING

In addition to modeling, many strategy training interventions, including some of those referenced previously, have also included prompts or cues to facilitate strategy use. These prompts, or cues, can be either fixed (i.e., the prompts that are embedded into a task do not change over time)[154] or adaptive (i.e., the level of prompting or cueing changes or disappears as learners improve their task performance).[155] Prompts or cues can be as simple as an oral reminder to remember to use a certain strategy or a set of strategies, or in a more complex scaffolding scheme. For example, exit slips (students' reflections on what they have learned at the end of class) can prompt students to engage in strategies such as summarization or connecting to prior knowledge. As with modeling discussed previously, prompting and cueing have been extensively investigated as training techniques for students with cognitive disabilities.[156]

Offered here are two such examples of prompting or cueing of strategy use in science and history. One typical task in chemistry class is balancing chemical equations. One domain-specific strategy to do this is to balance the pure nonmetallic elements (such as hydrogen and oxygen) first using fractional coefficients (such as $\frac{1}{2}$ or $\frac{3}{2}$). Then, after balancing, one can multiply each coefficient in the equation by the common denominator to return to whole-number coefficients. A teacher could employ a fixed prompt in the directions for

Instructional Principles 121

the assignment or before each problem to use this fractional coefficient method. A more adaptive approach would be to prompt only when the student appears to be unable to solve a particular chemical equation and entirely remove this prompt as the student becomes facile with this strategy or as this process becomes automatized (i.e., skillful).

In history, judging perspective is a crucial strategy during historical inquiry (discussed in depth in Chapter 9). Asking students to specifically examine who the source is and what their particular perspective may be every time the student includes a new source may need to be necessary. For example, after reading a letter by George Mason (Virginia delegate to the US Constitutional Convention) about the need for stronger language in the US Constitution about state control over militias, prompting the student to understand the viewpoint of Mason—who was a Southern slave owner—will shed light on his particular viewpoint. This viewpoint would differ from that of a Northern delegate, generally opposed to slavery. As learners were acclimating themselves in history, these prompts would likely need to be frequent and fixed, whereas they should be faded as the learner reaches the middle and upper stages of competence.

One of the difficulties of using an instructional approach such as prompting is trying to figure out when prompts should be offered, when these prompts need to be adjusted, and when those prompts need to be removed altogether. Vygotsky's zone of proximal development[157] has been used as a way to think about the introduction, adjustment, and removal of prompts (fading) and cues. The prompts should not be so rigid that the learner does not discover for herself which strategies to employ when, but instead gradually create the conditions to let her practice the strategies first with help—through the prompts—then remove this help over time so that the learner becomes self-regulatory in her efforts to use that strategy.[158]

It might be instructive to consider a physical example of strategy use before moving toward a more conceptual example. A toddler learning to pedal her tricycle may have difficulty getting started, particularly if the pedals are positioned parallel to the ground. Prompting that toddler to "pedal backward" a little, then pedaling forward when the pedals are no longer parallel with the ground, may be helpful. However, continuing to prompt this strategy may not always be wise. For instance, if there is a step behind that toddler, pedaling the tricycle backwards could be dangerous. Additionally, in order for the toddler to understand when pedaling backward is necessary and when it is not, she needs to have those experiences with implementing the strategy on her own.

A conceptual example could be learning to write text. One helpful prompt may be to start with a topic sentence. For a beginning writer, this prompt might be helpful a large majority of the time. However, as that writer becomes more proficient, this strategy might actually hinder their writing, particularly with narrative writing. Thus, the prompt to start with a topic sentence needs to be adjusted or faded to allow the writer to choose the most appropriate sentence construction for the task at hand—whether that be narrative, expository, or persuasive text.

MOTIVATION TO USE STRATEGIES

While the previous two instructional approaches were specific instructional strategies aimed directly at strategy use, intervening in ways to influence students' motivation for a task may have an indirect effect on students' strategy use, as discussed in Chapter 11. Most importantly, if students are not motivated to engage in a particular task, they are unlikely to be strategic in that process because by definition strategies are effortful processes. At best, students may fall back on more skillful types of processing that may be less effective in order to complete the task.

One motivational approach would be to foster the adoption of mastery goals (i.e., goals for learning), because students who adopt mastery goals typically use strategies more effectively than those who do not.[159] In addition, mastery goals typically result in more deep-level strategy use.[160] External rewards for completing a task are more likely to foster extrinsic goals for a task (i.e., performance goals),[161] therefore not offering external rewards may actually help students adopt more mastery goals, or at the very least not encourage the adoption of performance goals. For example, allowing students to practice addition without the promise of some reward, such as a sticker, may induce more strategy use if they choose to adopt mastery goals rather than performance goals.

MAKE SURE STRATEGY USE IS MEANINGFUL AND EMBED THAT STRATEGY USE

Strategy instruction also needs to be implemented in ways that students see the value of the particular strategy being trained. If the student uses a strategy and it does not help, it is unlikely that strategy will be used again—particularly if the student is engaged metacognitively. In other words, it is not enough that children use strategies with a particular frequency, but they also need to use them appropriately—both in terms of how they use the strategy and when they use it.

Take for example the count-on strategy. Training a child to use the count-on strategy and having that strategy available is only the first step in making that strategy meaningful to that child. If that child cannot use that strategy in a quality way, that particular strategy will not help. For instance, if a child wants to add five and seven but they cannot correctly count-on seven with their fingers, the strategy is not a good one until they can correctly count on their fingers first. Additionally, if the child uses the strategies for inappropriate tasks—such as addition problem with addends over 10 or for subtraction problems—the strategy again is not meaningful. If the explanation in Overlapping Waves Theory (OWT) is correct, that student who is monitoring appropriately will stop using that particular strategy.[10] Thus, it is crucial that all three aspects of strategy use are attended to as strategies are trained.

Part of making strategy use meaningful may include embedding that strategy use in meaningful activities or tasks. Tailoring strategy use and the instruction of those strategies with regard to individuals' strengths and weaknesses as well as the nature of the task at hand are crucial.[162] Embedding strategy use in meaningful tasks may also help support some of the motivational constructs suggested in the preceding section.

FOCUS ON A FEW STRATEGIES AT A TIME

It is important not to overwhelm students with too many strategies at one time. Given the relatively small effects of shorter-term strategy training, focusing on the most critical strategies and spending more time with these important strategies is more likely to leave a lasting impact on that student's strategy use. Recall that learners in acclimation in a domain typically have more fragmented knowledge, meaning that their domain knowledge lacks coherence.[163] Because this domain knowledge includes knowledge of strategies, these learners also lack the principled knowledge (interconnected stores of knowledge)[164] to understand how to coordinate their prior knowledge and strategy use in meaningful ways.

For example, focusing on all 30-plus reading behaviors identified by Pressley and Afflerbach[45] in the course of one month may expose students to a lot of potential strategies, however, it is unlikely that they will be able to use any one strategy particularly well (i.e., it will be particularly useful or used in a conditional manner). Instructionally, training for usefulness and conditionality will likely involve demonstrating (through some of the instructional strategies described earlier) a particular strategy enough times so that students can use it well and at the appropriate times. For instance, **visualizing** might be a helpful strategy for students in Florida who are reading about the beach, but it might not be a good strategy for those same students when reading about a blizzard, because they might not have the prior knowledge or experience to visualize it in ways that are particularly helpful.

THREE PRINCIPLES OF EFFECTIVE STRATEGY INSTRUCTION

Three principles of strategy instruction suggested by Harris and Pressley[165] may help guide teachers and instructors in the use of these instructional approaches. These principles are that cognitive instruction is an emerging approach, there is not a set of cure-all strategies, and that good strategy instruction is not rote.

First, with regard to an emerging approach, it is important to keep in mind that strategy instruction is continuously revised. Like the discussion on adjusting or fading cues previously, the approaches used to teach effective strategies have to change in light of the individuals' performance. One approach is not likely to work for all individuals across time, rather certain approaches may work at certain times for certain individuals. It is the role of the instructor to use assessment data to determine which approaches have worked for which situations and apply that to future situations, always adjusting as needed.

Just as instructional approaches to teaching strategies adapt and change over time, the strategies that are taught must also change all the time. As the Model of Domain Learning (MDL) and OWT suggest that strategy use will change and develop over time, caution must be exercised as suggesting to individuals that a certain strategy or strategies will "always work." The particular suggested strategy has to be matched to both the child *and* the task.

Finally, good strategy instruction is not rote. For those who consider strategies as purposeful and conscious, the routinization of strategies does not help train new strategies or their effective use. Rote learning or memorization may be appropriate for certain types of well-structured tasks—such as saving data in a spreadsheet program—but might be ill-suited to many ill-structured tasks. While being able to employ a strategy is useful, and rote learning may be effective at this, being able to know how and why that strategy works is essential for helping the individual become self-regulated in their strategy use.

ADDITIONAL READINGS

Harris, K.R., & Pressley, M. (1991). The nature of cognitive strategy instruction: Interactive strategy instruction. *Exceptional Children, 57*, 392–404.

> *This article discusses effective strategy instruction and argues that facets of strategy instruction typically in the literature aligned well with constructivist frameworks. The*

authors use multiple examples in different domains of strategy instruction and argue that strategy instruction should support both cognitive strategies themselves, as well as support for individuals' self-regulation.

Ramdass, D., & Zimmerman, B.J. (2008). Effects of self-correction strategy training on middle school students' self-efficacy, self-evaluation, and mathematics division learning. *Journal of Advanced Academics*, 20, 18–41.

The authors describe a specific mathematics strategy training program for middle-school students in mathematics. This program relied on many of the motivational elements discussed in the current chapter, including self-efficacy. Additionally, the strategy training program emphasizes some domain-general strategies, such as self-checking, that could be used in domains other than mathematics.

Sung, Y.T., Chang, K.E., & Huang, J.S. (2008). Improving children's reading comprehension and use of strategies through computer-based strategy training. *Computers in Human Behavior*, 24, 1552–1571.

This article offers a specific example of a strategy training model based on previous information-processing models. It consists of a system that facilitates the use of multiple strategies. Further, the facilitation of strategy use is given via a computerized system—the Computer Assisted Strategy Teaching and Learning Environment (CASTLE).

Hassan, X., Macaro, E., Mason, D., Nye, G., Smith, P., & Vanderplank, R. (2005). *Strategy training in language learning—a systematic review of available research*. London: EPPI-Centre, Social Science Research Unit, Institute of Education, University of London. Retrieved from: http://eppi.ioe.ac.uk/cms/Portals/0/PDF%20reviews%20and%20summaries/mfl_rv1.pdf?ver=2006-03-02-124956-547

This systematic review examines the effects of strategy training on language learning. While the authors conclude that strategy training for language learning can be quite effective, they also caution that the strategy training studies that they examined were quite diverse and that it was difficult to determine how to generalize strategy training across the different studies they reviewed.

Glossary

activating background knowledge	a writing strategy to recall information from memory that is useful for the current text being written.
analogy	understanding patterns in data by comparing those data to other data that have a similar structure.
anomaly	understanding patterns in data by locating data that differs from the overall pattern.
antinomy	understanding patterns in data by identifying incompatibilities to rule out possible conclusions.
antithesis	understanding patterns in data by observing the contrary effects of the same action in two different circumstances.
arguing with text	a reading strategy where the reader tries to refute an argument the author has made.
autonomous motivation	motivation to complete a task based on interest or enjoyment in the task or its relation to one's personal goals.
chunking	a working memory strategy where an individual recognizes a familiar pattern to rapidly encode that pattern into working memory as one chunk, rather than discrete pieces of information.

clumping a mathematics strategy where the measure of central tendency is estimated by finding the largest "clump" of numbers.

cognitive strategies strategies that are invoked to actually solve a problem or learn more about a topic.

compare and contrast a historical inquiry strategy of finding the similarities and differences between two historical events or descriptions of those historical events.

concept maps a graphical organizational strategy that consists of a central concept, related concepts, and linkages between those relating concepts using lines or arrows in addition to propositions that describe those relations.

connecting to personal experience a reading strategy where the reader uses past experiences to make sense of a new text.

consistency checking an epistemic strategy to determine if information is congruent with or justified by other information presented.

control of variables a science strategy where the individual manipulates one input variable at a time to see the effect on one or more output variables.

controlled motivation motivation to complete a task based on either receiving a reward or punishment or due to feelings of guilt, shame, or anxiety.

count-all a mathematics addition strategy where children use their fingers to represent addends.

count-back a mathematics subtraction strategy where children use one hand to represent the subtrahend.

Glossary

count-on a mathematics addition strategy where children use one hand to represent a smaller addend.

decomposition breaking a mathematics problem down into smaller subcomponents, such as solving a division problem through a series of subtractions.

deductive reasoning using a general rule that has been learned systematically.

deep-level strategies strategies that are aimed at more extensive manipulations or transformation of a problem or task.

directly recalling propositions a writing strategy of recalling information directly from long-term memory.

direct translation an L2 writing strategy where translated words are directly retrieved from long-term memory.

domain-general strategies strategies that can be employed effectively in any task, regardless of the academic domain.

domain knowledge breadth and scope of subject-matter knowledge in a particular academic domain.

domain-specific strategies strategies that can be employed effectively only in a particular academic domain.

dot-notation a mathematics arithmetic strategy where dots on Arabic numbers are used to help add and subtract numbers.

elaboration a reading strategy where the reader uses their own prior knowledge to build understanding that may be tangential to the text.

enacting a generative strategy where the individual "acts out" material or information.

epistemic strategies — strategies aimed at reflecting on the limits, certainty, and criteria of knowing.

evaluating agreement with text — a strategy where the reader evaluates their own stance and the author's stance about a particular topic.

evaluating comprehension — a reading strategy where the reader monitors their understanding of a particular text.

evaluating interest — a reading strategy where the reader monitors their level of interest in a particular text.

evaluating text quality — a reading strategy where the reader makes a judgment about the merit of the text itself.

evaluating the importance of text — a reading strategy where the reader makes a judgment about the relative importance of a piece of text.

evaluating the quality of the argument — a reading strategy where the reader makes a judgment about the quality of the overall argument made by the author.

expressing amusement — a reading behavior where the reader expresses feelings of enjoyment or pleasure.

expressing surprise — a reading behavior where the reader expresses feelings of sympathy toward another.

field observation strategies — science strategies that involve important features of a problem, usually those that involve geologic features.

formative assessment — the use of student data to drive instructional or curricular decisions.

global restatement — a reading strategy where the reader paraphrases or repeats information between multiple paragraphs.

Glossary

graphic organizers an organizational strategy that uses drawing to show spatial relations about how different concepts are related in a linear or non-linear manner.

guessing the meaning of a word in context a reading strategy of using the words around an unknown word to better understand the meaning of the text or a specific word.

help seeking identifying and using environmental resources to improve learning or task performance.

heuristics rules of thumb that are not always the most efficient or effective way to solve a problem.

highlighting an attentional strategy where individuals mark what they perceive to be important text by using a highlighter to color that text.

historical simulations using historical problems to isolate key features of a problem by having individuals act these problems out (e.g., Model UN).

history-cued strategy a science strategy where the individual uses a hypothesis to systematically test the effect of multiple input variables on one or more output variables.

identifying a potential audience the writing strategy of matching who the writing is for and the writer's message.

ill-structured tasks or problems tasks or problems that have more than one correct answer or multiple ways to reach those correct answers (i.e., not well structured).

improving the clarity of writing a writing strategy to ensure there is flow to the argument or alignment in plot elements.

individual interest	sustained disposition toward an academic domain, topic, or content area.
inductive reasoning	using particular experiences an individual has to develop a general rule.
instrumental goals	goals learners create that are either intrinsic or extrinsic that motivate them to complete a specific task.
interpreting	a reading strategy where the reader uses a reasoning process to integrate text into their own situation model.
knowledge-based validation	an epistemic strategy of using what one already knows to determine if new information is plausible or true.
learning	a change in one's mental schema (the structure and organization of one's knowledge).
local restatement	a reading strategy where the reader paraphrases or repeats information at the sentence or paragraph level.
making connections to background knowledge	a reading strategy where the reader tries to better understand a text by linking that text to knowledge they already have.
making connections to prior text	a reading strategy where the reader uses previous textual material to make sense of the text they are currently reading.
metacognitive strategies	strategies aimed at monitoring or controlling the cognitive strategies that have been employed.
method of loci	a type of mnemonic where new information is mapped onto existing information that occurs in some series of unfamiliar objects to familiar objects.

Glossary

mnemonics	an elaborative strategy where new information is mapped onto existing information in memory, such as an acronym.
negative activating emotions	emotions like anger that increase cognitive processing, but not necessarily deeper-level processing.
negative deactivating emotions	emotions like boredom that decrease cognitive processing.
notetaking	an organizational strategy to capture information from the environment in some idiosyncratic way.
number-line strategies	using a number line as a representational aid in arithmetic calculations.
number series	a mathematics multiplication strategy that uses repeated addition.
organizing thoughts and ideas	a writing strategy in which the writer plans the systematic manner in which they will express their ideas.
outlining	an organization strategy to list concepts and mark how subordinate concepts are related to those main concepts.
pictorial strategies	mathematics strategies that rely on visual-spatial properties of drawings or objects.
positive activating emotions	emotions like enjoyment that increase deeper-level cognitive processing.
positive deactivating emotions	emotions like relief that decrease cognitive processing.
predicting the micro- or macro-structure of the text	a reading strategy where the reader guesses what the forthcoming text is about to say.
prospective self-report	measure or measurements of strategy processing that occur before a given task.

Glossary

questioning — a reading strategy where the reader asks themselves a question to prompt their own thinking.

reading aloud — a reading strategy where a reader reads aloud a portion or all of a text to better understand that text.

rehearsal — a working memory strategy where an individual repeats information to maintain that information in working memory.

rereading — a reading strategy where the reader reads again a portion or all of a text to better understand it.

retrospective self-report — measures or measurements of strategic processing that occur after a given task, usually a Likert-type measure.

self-directed photo documentation — using photographic evidence to interpret events from multiple perspectives.

self-explanation — an elaborative strategy where individuals generate their own explanations about the material being studied during or after a task.

self-questioning — an elaborative strategy where individuals generate their own questions about a task or a problem.

situational interest — externally triggered, task-specific interest.

skills — a special form of procedural knowledge that is automatic, habitual, effortless, and used to make progress on a given problem or learning task.

skimming — a reading strategy where the reader skips over portions of the text.

Glossary

source work
identification, attribution, perspective judgment, and reliability assessments of primary and secondary sources.

strategies
a special form of procedural knowledge that is purposeful, intentional, effortful, used to acquire new knowledge, transfer knowledge to other problems, or transform a problem.

structured interviews
a measure of strategies processing that uses a standard set of open-ended questions about cognitive processing.

studying
cognitive engagement that the learner uses to perform better on a task or test they are about to take.

summarizing
an organizational strategy where the individual identifies the main idea or supporting details in their own words.

summative assessment
the use of student data to describe a student's past academic achievement.

surface-level strategies
strategies that are aimed at trying to understand a given problem or task.

symbolic strategies
mathematics strategies that rely on symbols or combinations of symbols.

teaching
a generative strategy where an individual explains material or information to someone else.

topic knowledge
depth of knowledge about specific content within an academic domain.

underlining
an attentional strategy where individuals mark what they perceive to be important text by drawing a line underneath that text.

using a text feature	a reader strategy whereby a reader uses some organizing feature—such as a table or a heading—to better understand that text.
using synonyms	an L2 writing strategy where a writer substitutes a synonym for an unfamiliar or uncertain word.
visualizing fractions	a mathematics strategy where pictorial graphs are used to help compare different fractional values.
well-structured tasks or problems	tasks or problems that have one correct answer and one or a few specific ways to achieve that correct answer.

References

1 Alexander, P.A., Grossnickle, E.M., Dumas, D., & Hattan, C. (in press). A retrospective and prospective examination of cognitive strategies and academic development: Where have we come in twenty-five years? In A. O'Donnell (Ed.), *Handbook of educational psychology*. Oxford: Oxford University Press.
2 Afflerbach, P., Pearson, P.D., & Paris, S.G. (2008). Clarifying differences between reading skills and reading strategies. *Reading Teacher*, 61, 364–373.
3 Kitchner, K.S. (1983). Cognition, metacognition, and epistemic cognition. *Human Development*, 26, 222–232.
4 Flavell, J.H. (1979). Metacognition and cognitive monitoring: A new area of cognitive-developmental inquiry. *American Psychologist*, 34, 906–911.
5 Marton, F., & Säljö, R. (1976). On qualitative differences in learning: I—outcome and process*. *British Journal of Educational Psychology*, 46, 4–11.
6 Richardson, J.T. (2015). Approaches to learning or levels of processing: What did Marton and Säljö (1976a) really say? The legacy of the work of the Göteborg group in the 1970s. *Interchange*, 46, 239–269.
7 Alexander, P.A., Sperl, C.T., Buehl, M.M., Fives, H., & Chiu, S. (2004). Modeling domain learning: Profiles from the field of special education. *Journal of Educational Psychology*, 96, 545–557.
8 Craik, F.I., & Lockhart, R.S. (1972). Levels of processing: A framework for memory research. *Journal of Verbal Learning and Verbal Behavior*, 11, 671–684.
9 Biggs, J.B. (1978). Individual and group differences in study processes. *British Journal of Educational Psychology*, 48, 266–279.
10 Siegler, R.S. (1996). *Emerging minds: The process of change in children's thinking*. New York: Oxford University Press.

References

11 Askeland, M. (2012). Sound-based strategy training in multiplication. *European Journal of Special Needs Education*, 27, 201–217.

12 Piaget, J. (1977). *The development of thought: Equilibration of cognitive structures.* Oxford: Viking.

13 Boaler, J. (1993). The role of contexts in the mathematics classroom: Do they make mathematics more "real"? *For the Learning of Mathematics*, 13, 12–17.

14 Alexander, P.A. (1997). Mapping the multidimensional nature of domain learning: The interplay of cognitive, motivational, and strategic forces. In M.L. Maehr & P.R. Pintrich (Eds.), *Advances in motivation and achievement* (Vol. 10, pp. 213–250). Greenwich, CT: JAI Press.

15 Alexander, P.A., Murphy, P.K., Woods, B.S., Duhon, K.E., & Parker, D. (1997). College instruction and concomitant changes in students' knowledge, interest, and strategy use: A study of domain learning. *Contemporary Educational Psychology*, 22, 125–146. doi:10.1006/ceps.1997.0927

16 Hidi, S., & Renninger, K.A. (2006). The four-phase model of interest development. *Educational Psychologist*, 41, 111–127. doi:10.1207/s15326985ep4102_4

17 Berliner, D.C. (1994). Expertise: The wonders of exemplary performance. In J.N. Mangieri & C.C. Block (Eds.), *Creating powerful thinking in teachers and students* (pp. 141–186). Fort Worth, TX: Holt, Rinehart and Winston.

18 Alexander, P.A. (2004). A model of domain learning: Reinterpreting expertise as a multidimensional, multistage process. In D.Y. Dai & R.J. Sternberg (Eds.), *Motivation, emotion, and cognition: Integrative perspectives on intellectual functioning and development* (pp. 273–298). Mahwah, NJ: Lawrence Erlbaum Associates.

19 Simon, H.A. (1978). Information-processing theory of human problem solving. In W.K. Estes (Ed.), *Handbook of learning and cognitive processes* (pp. 271–295). Hillsdale, NJ: Lawrence Erlbaum Associates.

20 Winne, P.H., & Hadwin, A.F. (1998). Studying as self-regulated learning. In D.J. Hacker, J. Dunlosky, & A.C. Graesser (Eds.), *Metacognition in educational theory and practice* (pp. 277–304). Mahwah, NJ: Lawrence Erlbaum.

21 Dinsmore, D.L., Grossnickle, E.M., & Dumas, D. (2017). Learning to study strategically. In R.E. Mayer & P.A. Alexander (Eds.), *Handbook*

References   141

of research on learning and teaching: Second edition (pp. 207–232). New York: Routledge.

22 Hartley, J., Bartlett, S., & Branthwaite, A. (1980). Underlining can make a difference—sometimes. *Journal of Educational Research*, 73, 218–224.

23 Shrager, L., & Mayer, R. E. (1989). Note-taking fosters generative learning strategies in novices. *Journal of Educational Psychology*, 81, 263–264.

24 Kiewra, K. A. (1989). A review of note-taking: The encoding-storage paradigm and beyond. *Educational Psychology Review*, 1, 147–172.

25 Darch, C., & Gersten, R. (1986). Direction-setting activities in reading comprehension: A comparison of two approaches. *Learning Disability Quarterly*, 9, 235–243.

26 Waller, R., & Whalley, P. (1987). Graphically organized prose. In E. de Corte (Ed.), *Learning and instruction: European research in an international context* (pp. 369–381). Leuven, Belgium: Leuven University Press.

27 Robinson, D. H., & Kiewra, K. A. (1995). Visual argument: Graphic organizers are superior to outlines in improving learning from text. *Journal of Educational Psychology*, 87, 455–467.

28 Novak, J. (1991). Clarify with concept maps. *Science Teacher*, 58, 44–49.

29 Ruiz-Primo, M. A., & Shavelson, R. J. (1996). Problems and issues in the use of concept maps in science assessment. *Journal of Research in Science Teaching*, 33, 569–600.

30 Atkinson, R. C., & Raugh, M. R. (1975). An application of the mnemonic keyword method to the acquisition of a Russian vocabulary. *Journal of Experimental Psychology: Human Learning and Memory*, 1, 126.

31 Verhaeghen, P., & Marcoen, A. (1996). On the mechanisms of plasticity in young and older adults after instruction in the method of loci: Evidence for an amplification model. *Psychology and Aging*, 11, 164–178.

32 King, A. (1992). Comparison of self-questioning, summarizing, and notetaking-review as strategies for learning from lectures. *American Educational Research Journal*, 29, 303–323.

33 Chi, M. T., Bassok, M., Lewis, M. W., Reimann, P., & Glaser, R. (1989). Self-explanations: How students study and use examples in learning to solve problems. *Cognitive Science*, 13, 145–182.

34 Rittle-Johnson, B. (2006). Promoting transfer: Effects of self-explanation and direct instruction. *Child Development*, 77, 1–15.

35 Craik, F. I., & Watkins, M. J. (1973). The role of rehearsal in short-term memory. *Journal of Verbal Learning and Verbal Behavior*, 12, 599–607.

References

36 Chase, W.G., & Simon, H.A. (1973). Perception in chess. *Cognitive Psychology, 4,* 55–81.

37 Gobet, F., & Simon, H.A. (1998). Expert chess memory: Revisiting the chunking hypothesis. *Memory, 6,* 225–255.

38 Fiorella, L., & Mayer, R.E. (2015). *Learning as a generative activity: Eight learning strategies that promote understanding.* New York: Cambridge University Press.

39 Aleven, V., Stahl, E., Schworm, S., Fischer, F., & Wallace, R. (2003). Help seeking and help design in interactive learning environments. *Review of Educational Research, 73,* 277–320.

40 Ryan, A.M., & Pintrich, P.R. (1998). Achievement and social motivation influences on help seeking in the classroom. In S.A. Karabenick (Ed.), *Strategic help seeking: Implications for learning and teaching* (pp. 117–139). Mahwah, NJ: Lawrence Erlbaum Associates.

41 Dinsmore, D.L. (2017). Towards a dynamic, multidimensional model of strategic processing. *Educational Psychology Review, 29,* 235–268. doi: 10.1007/s10648-017-9407-5.

42 Hadwin, A.F., Winne, P.H., Stockley, D.B., Nesbit, J.C., & Woszczya, C. (2001). Context moderates students' self-reports about how they study. *Journal of Educational Psychology, 93,* 477–487.

43 Webb, S. (2002). *If the universe is teeming with aliens ... where is everybody? Fifty solutions to the Fermi paradox and the problem of extraterrestrial life.* New York: Copernicus Books.

44 RAND Reading Study Group. (2002). *Reading for understanding: Toward an R&D program in reading comprehension.* Santa Monica, CA: RAND.

45 Pressley, M., & Afflerbach, P. (1995). *Verbal protocols of reading: The nature of constructively responsive reading.* Hillsdale, NJ: Lawrence Erlbaum Associates.

46 Dinsmore, D.L., & Alexander, P.A. (2016). A multidimensional investigation of deep-level and surface-level processing. *Journal of Experimental Education, 84,* 213–244. doi: 10.1080/00220973.2014.979126

47 Kintsch, W. (2004). The construction-integration model of text comprehension and its implications for instruction. In R.B. Ruddell & N.J. Unrau (Eds.), *Theoretical models and processes of reading* (5th ed., pp. 1270–1362). Newark, DE: International Reading Association.

References

48 Ardoin, S.P., Williams, J.C., Klubnik, C., & McCall, M. (2009). Three versus six rereadings of practice passages. *Journal of Applied Behavioral Analysis*, 42, 375–380. doi:10.1901/jaba.2009.42-375

49 Levy, B.A., Di Persio, R., & Hollingshead, A. (1992). Fluent rereading: Repetition, automaticity, and discrepancy. *Journal of Experimental Psychology*, 18, 957–971.

50 Garner, R., Gillingham, M.G., & White, C.S. (1989). Effects of 'seductive details' on macroprocessing and microprocessing in adults and children. *Cognition and Instruction*, 6, 41–57.

51 Alexander, P.A. (2005). The path to competence: A lifespan developmental perspective on reading. *Journal of Literacy Research*, 37, 413–436.

52 Dinsmore, D.L., Fox, E., Parkinson, M.M., & Rahman, T. (2010, May). A deeper look at why readers succeed or fail. In D. McNamara (Chair), *Integration, depth, and complexity: Characterizing reader types through multidimensional profiling*. Symposium presented at the annual meeting of the American Educational Research Association, Denver.

53 Fox, E., Dinsmore, D.L., & Alexander, P.A. (2010). Reading competence, interest, and reading goals in three gifted young adolescent readers. [Special Issue on Motivation and giftedness]. *High Ability Studies*, 21, 165–178. doi:10.1080/13598139.2010.525340

54 Dinsmore, D.L., & Parkinson, M.M. (2016, July). Investigating the relations between high school students' depth of processing and metacognitive strategy use. In D.L. Dinsmore & L. Fryer (Chairs), *The intersection between depth and the regulation of strategy use*. Symposium presented at the Higher Education Conference, Amsterdam, Netherlands.

55 Fox, E., Dinsmore, D.L., Maggioni, L., & Alexander, P.A. (2009, April). *Undergraduates reading of course texts*. Paper presented at the annual meeting of the American Educational Research Association, San Diego.

56 Flower, L., & Hayes, J.R. (1981). A cognitive process theory of writing. *College Composition and Communication*, 32, 365–387.

57 Harris, K.R., Graham, S., & Mason, L. (2002). OSEP research institutes: Bridging research and practice POW plus TREE equals powerful opinion. *Teaching Exceptional Children*, 34, 74.

58 Harris, K.R., Graham, S., & Mason, L.H. (2003). Self-regulated strategy development in the classroom: Part of a balanced approach to writing instruction for students with disabilities. *Focus on Exceptional Children*, 35, 1–16.

References

59 Graham, S., & Harris, K.R. (2003). Students with learning disabilities and the process of writing: A meta-analysis of SRSD studies. In H.L. Swanson, K.R. Harris, & S. Graham (Eds.), *Handbook of learning disabilities* (pp. 323–344). New York: Guilford Press.

60 He, T.H., Chang, S.M., & Chen, S.H.E. (2011). Multiple goals, writing strategies, and written outcomes for college students learning English as a second language. *Perceptual and Motor Skills*, 112, 401–416.

61 Greeno, J.G., & Simon, H.A. (1988). Problem solving and reasoning. In R.C. Atkinson, R. Herrnstein, G. Lindzey, & R.D. Luce (Eds.), *Steven's handbook of experimental psychology* (rev. ed., pp. 589–672). New York: John Wiley & Sons.

62 Russell, B. (2001). *The problems of philosophy*. Oxford: Oxford University Press.

63 Murray, T.E., & Simon, B.L. (2002). At the intersection of regional and social dialects: The case of like past participle in American English. *American Speech*, 77, 32–69.

64 Lakoff, G. (1965). *On the nature of syntactic irregularity*. Unpublished doctoral dissertation, Harvard University.

65 Woods-Groves, S., Therrien, W.J., Hua, Y., & Hendrickson, J.M. (2013). Essay-writing strategy for students enrolled in a postsecondary program for individuals with developmental disabilities. *Remedial and Special Education*, 34, 131–141.

66 Pólya, G. (1957). *How to solve it: A new aspect of mathematical method*. London: Penguin.

67 Gick, M.L., & Holyoak, K.J. (1980). Analogical problem solving. *Cognitive Psychology*, 12, 306–355.

68 Schoenfeld, A.H. (1983). Episodes and executive decisions in mathematical problem solving. In R.A. Lesh & M. Landau (Eds.), *Acquisitions of mathematics concepts and processes* (pp. 345–395). New York: Academic Press.

69 Stylianou, D.A., & Silver, E.A. (2004). The role of visual representations in advanced mathematical problem solving: An examination of expert-novice similarities and differences. *Mathematical Thinking and Learning*, 6, 353–387.

70 Zazkis, R., Dubinsky, E., & Dautermann, J. (1996). Coordinating visual and analytic strategies: A study of students' understanding of the group D 4. *Journal for Research in Mathematics Education*, 27, 435–457.

References

71 Kingma, J., & Zumbo, B. (1988). Implicit ordinal number knowledge tasks as predictors for number line comprehension: A validation study. *Educational and Psychological Measurement*, 48, 219–230.

72 Demaree, D., Stonebraker, S., Zhao, W., & Bao, L. (2004). *Virtual reality in introductory physics laboratories*. Proceedings of the 2004 Physics Education Research Conference, Sacramento, CA.

73 Zhang, L., Goh, C.C., & Kunnan, A.J. (2014). Analysis of test takers' metacognitive and cognitive strategy use and EFL reading test performance: A multi-sample SEM approach. *Language Assessment Quarterly*, 11, 76–102.

74 Groen, G.J., & Poll, M. (1973). Subtraction and the solution of open sentence problems. *Journal of Experimental Child Psychology*, 16, 292–302.

75 Groth, R.E. (2005). An investigation of statistical thinking in two different contexts: Detecting a signal in a noisy process and determining a typical value. *Journal of Mathematical Behavior*, 24, 109–124.

76 Fazio, L.K., DeWolf, M., & Siegler, R.S. (2016). Strategy use and strategy choice in fraction magnitude comparison. *Journal of Experimental Psychology: Learning, Memory, and Cognition*, 42, 1–16.

77 Carpenter, T.P., & Moser, J.M. (1984). The acquisition of addition and subtraction concepts in grades one through three. *Journal for Research in Mathematics Education*, 15, 179–202.

78 Carr, M., & Alexeev, N. (2011). Fluency, accuracy, and gender predict developmental trajectories of arithmetic strategies. *Journal of Educational Psychology*, 103, 617–631.

79 Anderson, J.R. (1983). *The architecture of cognition*. Cambridge, MA: Harvard University Press.

80 Koedinger, K.R., & Tabachneck, H.J. (1994). *Two strategies are better than one: Multiple strategy use in word problem solving*. Annual meeting of the American Educational Research Association, New Orleans, LA.

81 Jitendra, A.K., Griffin, C.C., Haria, P., Leh, J., Adams, A., & Kaduvettoor, A. (2007). A comparison of single and multiple strategy instruction on third-grade students' mathematical problem solving. *Journal of Educational Psychology*, 99, 115–127.

82 Climate Interactive. (2016). C-learn climate simulator. Retrieved from: www.climateinteractive.org/tools/c-learn/simulation/

83 Taasoobshirazi, G., & Farley, J. (2013). A multivariate model of physics problem solving. *Learning and Individual Differences*, 24, 53–62.

References

84 Leopold, C., Sumfleth, E., & Leutner, D. (2013). Learning with summaries: Effects of representation mode and type of learning activity on comprehension and transfer. *Learning and Instruction*, 27, 40–49.

85 Ainsworth, S., Prain, V., & Tytler, R. (2011). Drawing to learn in science. *Science*, 333(6046), 1096–1097.

86 Künsting, J., Wirth, J., & Paas, F. (2011). The goal specificity effect on strategy use and instructional efficiency during computer-based scientific discovery learning. *Computers & Education*, 56, 668–679.

87 Kuhn, D. (2007). Reasoning about multiple variables: Control of variables is not the only challenge. *Science Education*, 91, 710–726.

88 Künsting, J., Kempf, J., & Wirth, J. (2013). Enhancing scientific discovery learning through metacognitive support. *Contemporary Educational Psychology*, 38, 349–360.

89 Liben, L.S., Kastens, K.A., & Christensen, A.E. (2011). Spatial foundations of science education: The illustrative case of instruction on introductory geological concepts. *Cognition and Instruction*, 29, 45–87.

90 Jonassen, D.H., Myers, J.M., & McKillop, A.M. (1996). From constructivism to constructionism: Learning with hypermedia/multimedia rather than from it. In B.G. Wilson (Ed.), *Constructivist learning environments: Case studies in instructional design* (pp. 93–106). Englewood Cliffs, NJ: Educational Technology.

91 Sullivan, S., Gnesdilow, D., & Puntambekar, S. (2011). Navigation behaviors and strategies used by middle school students to learn from a science hypertext. *Journal of Educational Multimedia and Hypermedia*, 20, 387.

92 Merchie, E., & Van Keer, H. (2014). Using on-line and off-line measures to explore fifth and sixth graders' text-learning strategies and schematizing skills. *Learning and Individual Differences*, 32, 193–203.

93 Jairam, D., Kiewra, K.A., Kauffman, D.F., & Zhao, R. (2012). How to study a matrix. *Contemporary Educational Psychology*, 37, 128–135.

94 Alexander, P.A., & The Disciplined Reading and Learning Research Laboratory. (2012). Reading into the future: Competence for the 21st century. *Educational Psychologist*, 47, 259–280.

95 Dumas, D. (2016). Relational reasoning in science, medicine, and engineering. *Educational Psychology Review*, 1–23. doi:10.1007/s10648-016-9370-6

96 Salomon, G., & Perkins, D.N. (1989). Rocky roads to transfer: Rethinking mechanism of a neglected phenomenon. *Educational Psychologist*, 24, 113–142.

References

97 Chinn, C.A., & Brewer, W.F. (1993). The role of anomalous data in knowledge acquisition: A theoretical framework and implications for science instruction. *Review of Educational Research*, 63, 1–49.

98 Cole, M., & Wertsch, J.V. (1996). Beyond the individual-social antinomy in discussions of Piaget and Vygotsky. *Human Development*, 39, 250–256.

99 Kuhn, D., & Udell, W. (2007). Coordinating own and other perspectives in argument. Thinking and Reasoning, 13, 90–104.

100 American Association for the Advancement of Science. (1989). *Project 2061 blueprints for reform: Science, mathematics, and technology education*. New York: Oxford University Press.

101 Richter, T., & Schmid, S. (2010). Epistemological beliefs and epistemic strategies in self-regulated learning. *Metacognition and Learning*, 5, 47–65.

102 Collins, A., & Ferguson, W. (1993). Epistemic forms and epistemic games: Structures and strategies to guide inquiry. *Educational Psychologist*, 28, 25–42.

103 Seixas, P. (1996). Conceptualizing the growth of historical understanding. In D.R. Olson (Ed.), *The handbook of education and human development: New models of learning, teaching, and schooling* (pp. 765–783). Malden, MA: Blackwell.

104 VanSledright, B. (2004). What does it mean to think historically . . . and how do you teach it. *Social Education*, 68, 230–233.

105 Milson, A.J. (2002). The Internet and inquiry learning: Integrating medium and method in a sixth grade social studies classroom. *Theory & Research in Social Education*, 30, 330–353.

106 Bråten, I., Strømsø, H.I., & Britt, M.A. (2009). Trust matters: Examining the role of source evaluation in students' construction of meaning within and across multiple texts. *Reading Research Quarterly*, 44, 6–28.

107 List, A., & Alexander, P.A. (2015). Examining response confidence in multiple text tasks. *Metacognition and Learning*, 10, 407–436.

108 Lawless, K.A., & Brown, S.W. (2015). Developing scientific literacy skills through interdisciplinary, technology-based global simulations: GlobalEd 2. *Curriculum Journal*, 26, 268–289.

109 Lewison, M., Flint, A.S., & Van Sluys, K. (2002). Taking on critical literacy: The journey of newcomers and novices. *Language Arts*, 79, 382–392.

110 Nichols, A., Kinninment, D., & Leat, D. (2001). *More thinking through geography*. Cambridge: Chris Kingston.

References

111 Markwell, K.W. (2000). Photo-documentation and analyses as research strategies in human geography. *Australian Geographical Studies, 38*, 91–98.

112 Ali-Khan, C., & Siry, C. (2014). Sharing seeing: Exploring photo-elicitation with children in two different cultural contexts. *Teaching and Teacher Education, 37*, 194–207. doi:10.1016/j.tate.2013.08.004

113 McIntosh, D. (2001). The uses and limits of the model United Nations in an international relations classroom. *International Studies Perspectives, 2*, 269–280.

114 Ambrosio, T. (2006). Trying Saddam Hussein: Teaching international law through an undergraduate mock trial. *International Studies Perspectives, 7*, 159–171. doi:10.1111/j.1528-3585.2006.00237.x

115 Wineburg, S.S. (1991). Historical problem solving: A study of the cognitive processes used in the evaluation of documentary and pictorial evidence. *Journal of Educational Psychology, 83*, 73–87.

116 Kuhn, D., & Weinstock, M. (2002). What is epistemological thinking and why does it matter? In B.K. Hofer & P.R. Pintrich (Eds.), *Personal epistemology: The psychology of beliefs about knowledge and knowing* (pp. 121–144). Mahwah, NJ: Erlbaum.

117 Shen, B., & Chen, A. (2007). Examination of learning profiles in physical education. *Journal of Teaching in Physical Education, 26*, 145–160.

118 Shen, B., & Chen, A. (2006). Examining the interrelations among knowledge, interests, and learning strategies. *Journal of Teaching in Physical Education, 25*, 182–199.

119 Cho, Y., Weinstein, C.E., & Wicker, F. (2011). Perceived competence and autonomy as moderators of the effects of achievement goal orientations. *Educational Psychology, 31*, 393–411.

120 Chen, C.H., & Wu, I.C. (2012). The interplay between cognitive and motivational variables in a supportive online learning system for secondary physical education. *Computers & Education, 58*, 542–550.

121 Deci, E.L., & Ryan, R.M. (2000). The "what" and "why" of goal pursuits: Human needs and the self-determination of behavior. *Psychological Inquiry, 11*, 227–268.

122 Soenens, B., & Vansteenkiste, M. (2005). Antecedents and outcomes of self-determination in 3 life domains: The role of parents' and teachers' autonomy support. *Journal of Youth and Adolescence, 34*, 589–604.

123 Vansteenkiste, M., Simons, J., Lens, W., Soenens, B., & Matos, L. (2005). Examining the motivational impact of intrinsic versus extrinsic goal

References 149

framing and autonomy-supportive versus internally controlling communication style on early adolescents' academic achievement. *Child Development*, 76, 483–501.

124 Vansteenkiste, M., Sierens, E., Soenens, B., Luyckx, K., & Lens, W. (2009). Motivational profiles from a self-determination perspective: The quality of motivation matters. *Journal of Educational Psychology*, 101, 671–688.

125 Fryer, L.K., Ginns, P., & Walker, R. (2014). Between students' instrumental goals and how they learn: Goal content is the gap to mind. *British Journal of Educational Psychology*, 84, 612–630.

126 Vansteenkiste, M., Simons, J., Lens, W., Sheldon, K.M., & Deci, E.L. (2004). Motivating learning, performance, and persistence: The synergistic effects of intrinsic goal contents and autonomy-supportive contexts. *Journal of Personality and Social Psychology*, 87, 246–260.

127 Muis, K.R., & Franco, G.M. (2009). Epistemic beliefs: Setting the standards for self-regulated learning. *Contemporary Educational Psychology*, 34, 306–318.

128 Greene, J.A., Muis, K.R., & Pieschl, S. (2010). The role of epistemic beliefs in students' self-regulated learning with computer-based learning environments: Conceptual and methodological issues. *Educational Psychologist*, 45, 245–257.

129 Linnenbrink-Garcia, L., Patall, E.A., & Pekrun, R. (2016). Adaptive motivation and emotion in education research and principles for instructional design. *Policy Insights from the Behavioral and Brain Sciences*, 3, 228–236.

130 Pekrun, R., Goetz, T., Titz, W., & Perry, R.P. (2002). Academic emotions in students' self-regulated learning and achievement: A program of qualitative and quantitative research. *Educational Psychologist*, 37, 91–105. doi:10.1207/S15326985EP3702_4

131 Bruinsma, M. (2004). Motivation, cognitive processing and achievement in higher education. *Learning and Instruction*, 14, 549–568.

132 Pekrun, R., Goetz, T., Frenzel, A.C., Barchfeld, P., & Perry, R.P. (2011). Measuring emotions in students' learning and performance: The achievement emotions questionnaire (AEQ). *Contemporary Educational Psychology*, 36, 36–48. doi:10.1016/j.cedpsych.2010.10.002

133 Donovan, J.L., & Marshall, C.R. (2015). Comparing the verbal self-reports of spelling strategies used by children with and without dyslexia. *International Journal of Disability, Development and Education*, 63, 1–18.

References

134 Peters, S., Koolschijn, P.C.M., Crone, E.A., Van Duijvenvoorde, A.C., & Raijmakers, M.E. (2014). Strategies influence neural activity for feedback learning across child and adolescent development. *Neuropsychologia*, 62, 365–374.

135 Winke, P. (2013). An investigation into second language aptitude for advanced Chinese language learning. *Modern Language Journal*, 97, 109–130.

136 Alexander, P.A., & Murphy, P.K. (1998). Profiling the differences in students' knowledge, interest, and strategic processing. *Journal of Educational Psychology*, 90, 435–447.

137 Cleary, T.J., Callan, G.L., & Zimmerman, B.J. (2012). Assessing self-regulation as a cyclical, context-specific phenomenon: Overview and analysis of SRL microanalytic protocols. *Education Research International*. doi:10.1155/2012/428639

138 Veenman, M.V., Prins, F.J., & Verheij, J. (2003). Learning styles: Self-reports versus thinking-aloud measures. *British Journal of Educational Psychology*, 73, 357–372.

139 Ericsson, K.A., & Simon, H.A. (1998). How to study thinking in everyday life: Contrasting think-aloud protocols with descriptions and explanations of thinking. *Mind, Culture, and Activity*, 5, 178–186.

140 Moos, D.C., & Azevedo, R. (2008). Monitoring, planning, and self-efficacy during learning with hypermedia: The impact of conceptual scaffolds. *Computers in Human Behavior*, 24, 1686–1706.

141 Veenman, M.V., Van Hout-Wolters, B.H., & Afflerbach, P. (2006). Metacognition and learning: Conceptual and methodological considerations. *Metacognition and Learning*, 1, 3–14.

142 Dinsmore, D.L., Alexander, P.A., & Loughlin, S.M. (2008). Focusing the conceptual lens on metacognition, self-regulation, and self-regulated learning. *Educational Psychology Review*, 20, 391–409. doi:10.1007/s10648-008-9083-6

143 De Backer, L., Van Keer, H., & Valcke, M. (2012). Exploring the potential impact of reciprocal peer tutoring on higher education students' metacognitive knowledge and regulation. *Instructional Science*, 40, 559–588.

144 Popham, W.J. (2011). *Classroom assessment: What teachers need to know* (6th ed.). Boston, MA: Pearson.

145 Pintrich, P.R. (2002). The role of metacognitive knowledge in learning, teaching, and assessing. *Theory Into Practice*, 41, 219–225.

References

146 Vygotsky, L. (1978). *Mind in society.* Cambridge, MA: Harvard University Press.

147 Bandura, A. (1986). *Social foundations of thought and action: A social cognitive theory.* Englewood Cliffs, NJ: Prentice-Hall.

148 Rogoff, B. (1990). *Apprenticeship in thinking: Cognitive development in social context.* Oxford: Oxford University Press.

149 Meyer, B.J., & Poon, L.W. (2001). Effects of structure strategy training and signaling on recall of text. *Journal of Educational Psychology*, 93, 141–159.

150 Gist, M.E., Schwoerer, C., & Rosen, B. (1989). Effects of alternative training methods on self-efficacy and performance in computer software training. *Journal of Applied Psychology*, 74, 884–891.

151 McNamara, D.S., Levinstein, I.B., & Boonthum, C. (2004). iSTART: Interactive strategy training for active reading and thinking. *Behavior Research Methods, Instruments, & Computers*, 36, 222–233.

152 Schunk, D.H., & Cox, P.D. (1986). Strategy training and attributional feedback with learning disabled students. *Journal of Educational Psychology*, 78, 201–209.

153 Carrell, P.L., Pharis, B.G., & Liberto, J.C. (1989). Metacognitive strategy training for ESL reading. *TESOL Quarterly*, 23, 647–678.

154 Veenman, M.V., Kok, R., & Blöte, A.W. (2005). The relation between intellectual and metacognitive skills in early adolescence. *Instructional Science*, 33, 193–211.

155 Azevedo, R., Greene, J.A., & Moos, D.C. (2007). The effect of a human agent's external regulation upon college students' hypermedia learning. *Metacognition and Learning*, 2, 67–87.

156 Graham, S., & Freeman, S. (1986). Strategy training and teacher- vs. student-controlled study conditions: Effects on LD students' spelling performance. *Learning Disability Quarterly*, 9, 15–22.

157 Vygotsky, L. (1978). *Mind and society.* Cambridge, MA: Harvard University Press.

158 Meichenbaum, D. (1977). *Cognitive-behavior modification: An integrative approach.* New York: Plenum Press.

159 Ames, C., & Archer, J. (1988). Achievement goals in the classroom: Students' learning strategies and motivation processes. *Journal of Educational Psychology*, 80, 260–267.

160 Nolen, S.B. (1988). Reasons for studying: Motivational orientations and study strategies. *Cognition and Instruction*, 5, 269–287. doi:10.1207/s1532690xci0504_2

References

161 Deci, E.L., Koestner, R., & Ryan, R.M. (1999). A meta-analytic review of experiments examining the effects of extrinsic rewards on intrinsic motivation. *Psychological Bulletin, 125,* 627–668.

162 Harris, K.R. (1990). Developing self-regulated learners: The role of private speech and self-instructions. *Educational Psychologist, 25,* 35–50.

163 Alexander, P.A. (2003). The development of expertise: The journey from acclimation to proficiency. *Educational Researcher, 32,* 10–14.

164 Gelman. R., & Greeno, J.G. (1989). On the nature of competence: Principles for understanding in a domain. In L.B. Resnick (Ed.), *Knowing and learning: Essays in honor of Robert Glaser* (pp. 125–186). Hillsdale, NJ: Erlbaum.

165 Harris, K.R., & Pressley, M. (1991). The nature of cognitive strategy instruction: Interactive strategy construction. *Exceptional Children, 57,* 392–404.

Index

academic emotions, influence on strategy use 106–7
acclimation stage 20–3
acronyms, mnemonics and 29–30
activating background knowledge 57
agreement with text, evaluation of 47
amusement, expressing 48
analogy 86–7
anomaly 87
antinomy 87
antithesis 87
Approaches to Learning (Biggs) 12
argument: arguing with text 46; evaluating quality of 47
arithmetic strategies *see* mathematical strategies
assessment: formative 114–15; summative 114
attentional strategies 25–6
audience, identifying 56
autonomous motivation 103–4

background knowledge: activating 57; making connections to 44
Biggs' Approaches to Learning 12
bundling 35

cause and effect 94
challenged readers 49–50

chunking 32
CIM (Construction-Integration Model) 40
clarity of writing, improving 60
classification 94
clumping strategy 73
Cognitive-Motivational Model on the Effects of Emotions 106–7
Cognitive Process Model 53
cognitive strategies 9–10
common denominators, obtaining 75
compare and contrast 93
competence stage 20–3
competent readers 49
comprehension, evaluating 48
concept maps 29
concurrent self-report 112–13
conditionality, measurement of 109
connections, making: to background knowledge 44; to personal experience 45; to prior text 43
consistency checking 88–9
Construction-Integration Model (CIM) 40
context, guessing word meanings in 41–2
contrast 93

154 **Index**

controlled motivation 104
control of variables 82–3
count-all strategy 67–8
count-back strategy 4, 68
count-on strategy 68
critical literacy 94
cueing 120–2

dactylonomy 18
decision making, tactical 66–7
decomposition 72
deductive reasoning 59
deep-level strategies: definition of 11–12; for reading 44–7
denominators, common 75
development: of domain-general strategies 34–5; of mathematical strategies 76–9; of reading strategies 48–50; of science strategies 89; of social studies strategies 96–7; of strategic processing 15–23; of writing strategies 61–3
dictionaries, consulting 60
dips 84
directly recalling propositions 57
direct translation 60
domain-general strategies: attentional strategies 25–6; definition of 10–11, 24; development of 34–5; elaborative strategies 29–31; generative strategies 32–3; help-seeking strategies 33; heuristics 66; organizational strategies 26–9; working memory strategies 31–2
domain knowledge 19, 101
domain learning, use of skills and strategies in 5–8

domains, definition of 10
domain-specific strategies 11; *see also* mathematical strategies; reading strategies; science strategies; social studies strategies; writing strategies
dot-notation 69
drawing, representational 81

effortful processors 49
elaboration 47
elaborative strategies 29–31
ELLs (English language learners), modeling with 119
embedded strategy use 123–4
empathy, expressing 48
enacting 33
English language learners (ELLs), modeling with 119
epistemic strategies: about nature of science 88–9; definition of 10; influence on strategy use 105–6
evaluation: of agreement with text 47; of comprehension 48; of interest 48; of quality of argument 47; of text importance 43–4; of text quality 43; *see also* measurement
expertise, quest toward 20–3
expressing emotions 48

fading prompts 121–2
field observation strategies 84
finger counting 18
flashcards 34
formative assessment 114–15
fractions, visualizing 70–1
frameworks for strategic processing 15–16; Model of Domain

Index 155

Learning 18–23; Overlapping Waves Theory 16–18
frequency, measurement of 108–9

generative strategies 32–3
geography, strategies for 94–5
global restatements: definition of 42–3; in reading 45–6
goals, instrumental 104–5
government, strategies for 95
grammar, improving 59
graphic organizers 28
guessing word meanings in context 41–2

help-seeking strategies 33
heuristics 66
highlighting 25–6
historical inquiry 93–4
history cued strategy 83
How to Solve It: A New Aspect of Mathematical Method (Pólya) 65–6

identifying potential audience 56
ill-structured tasks 22
improving: clarity of writing 60; grammar, spelling, and punctuation 59
individual interest 19, 102
inductive reasoning 58
influences on strategy use: academic emotions 106–7; epistemic beliefs 105–6; interest 102–3; motivation 103–5; prior knowledge 101–2
inquiry-based strategies 82–3
instructional principles 117–18; embedded use 123–4; focusing on most critical strategies 124–5; meaningful use 123–4; modeling 118–20; motivational approaches 122–3; principles of 125–6; prompting/cueing 120–2
instrumental goals 104–5
interest: evaluation of 48; individual 19; influence on strategy use 102–3; interest reliant readers 49–50; situational 19
interest reliant readers 49–50
internalizing 12
interpreting 47
interviews 112

keyword method of mnemonics 29
knowledge 19; background knowledge 57; domain knowledge 19; knowledge-based validation 88; knowledge reliant readers 49–50; prior knowledge 101–2; topic knowledge 19
knowledge-based validation 88
knowledge reliant readers 49–50

L2 strategies 54, 60–1
learned skills 5
learned strategies 5
learning: attentional strategies 25–6; definition of 24–5; elaborative strategies 29–31; generative strategies 32–3; help-seeking strategies 33; organizational strategies 26–9; working memory strategies 31–2
linking words 29
local restatements 42
locations 94
loci, method of 30

Index

macrostructure of text, prediction of 43
maps, concept 29
Mason, George 121
mathematical strategies 65–7; development of 76–9; heuristics 66; pictorial strategies 67–71; symbolic strategies 67, 70–6
MDL *see* Model of Domain Learning (MDL), strategy measurement and 109
mean 74
measurement: aspects to measure 108–10; concurrent self-report 112–13; as formative evaluation 114–15; observations 113–14; prospective self-report 111; retrospective self-report 111; semi-structured interviews 112; structured interviews 112; *see also* evaluation
median 74
memorization: appropriateness of 126; deep-level strategy and 12
metacognitive strategies: definition of 10; for reading 47–8
method of loci 29
microstructure of text, prediction of 43
mnemonics 29–30
Mock Trial 95
modeling 118–20
Model of Domain Learning (MDL) 18–23; interest and 102; reading strategies and 48–50; science strategies and 89–90; social studies strategies and 96–7
Model UN 95
monitoring strategies 54–5

motivation: influence on strategy use 103–5; motivational strategy training 122–3
multiplying to obtain common denominators 75

nature of science, epistemic strategies about 88–9
negative activating emotions 106
negative deactivating emotions 106
NOS (nature of science), strategies about 88–9
notetaking 26–7
number-line strategies 70
number series strategy 68–9

observations 113–14
opposite-sides strategy 75–6
organizational strategies 26–9
organizing approach 12
outlining 27–8
Overlapping Waves Theory (OWT) 16–18; mathematical strategies and 76–9; reading strategies and 48; strategy measurement and 109; writing strategies and 61–3

personal experience, connecting to 45
photo documentation, self-directed 95
pictorial strategies: shift to symbolic strategies 77; types of 67–71
planning strategies 55–6
politics, strategies for 95
Pólya, George 65–6
positive activating emotions 106
positive deactivating emotions 106

Index 157

potential audience, identifying 56
POW writing model 53–4
predicting 43–4
prior knowledge, influence on strategy use 101–2
prior text, making connections to 43
problem solving, use of skills and strategies in 5–8
procedural knowledge 3–4
processing, types of 12
proficiency stage 20–3
prompting 120–2
propositions, recalling 57
prospective self-report 111
proximal development, zone of 121
punctuation, improving 59
Pythagoras's theorem 7

quality of argument, evaluation of 47
questioning: self-questioning 30–1; when reading 46

reading aloud 41
reading strategies 39–40; deep-level 44–7; development of 48–50; evaluative 47–8; metacognitive 47–8; surface-level 41–4
reasoning: deductive 59; inductive 58; relational 86–7
recalling propositions 57
rehearsal 31–2, 42
relational reasoning 86–7
representational drawing 81
reproducing 12
rereading 41
resistant readers 49–50

restatements: global 42–3, 45–6; local 42
retention of strategies 17–18
retrospective self-report 111
revising strategies 59–60
rote learning 126
Russell, Bertrand 58

schematics 84–5
schizophrenia: example graphic organizer for 28; example outline for 27
science strategies 80–2; development of 89; epistemic strategies 88–9; inquiry-based strategies 82–3; relational reasoning 86–7; schematics 84–5; spatial strategies 83–4
second language writing 54, 60–1
self-determination theory (SDT) 103
self-directed photo documentation 95
self-explanation 31
self-questioning 30–1
Self-Regulated Strategy Development (SRSD) model 54
self-report: concurrent 112–13; prospective 111; retrospective 111
semi-structured interviews 112
simulations 95
situational interest 19, 102–3
skillful behavior: definition of 4; in problem solving and domain learning 5–8
skills: definition of 4–5; development over time 5–6; learned skills 5; in problem solving and domain learning 5–8

skimming 41
social studies strategies 92–3; development of 96–7; for geography 94–5; government and politics 95; historical inquiry 93–4
source work 93–4
spatial recognition 84
spatial strategies 83–4
spelling, improving 59
SRSD (Self-Regulated Strategy Development) model 54
state-based strategies 13
strategic behavior: definition of 3–4; in problem solving and domain learning 5–8; *see also* strategy types
strategic-processing frameworks 15–16; Model of Domain Learning 18–23; Overlapping Waves Theory 16–18
strategy training 117–18; embedded use 123–4; focusing on most critical strategies 124–5; meaningful use 123–4; modeling 118–20; motivational approaches 122–3; principles of 125–6; prompting/cueing 120–2
strategy types: cognitive 9–10; deep-level 11–12; definition of 3–4, 24–5; developmental nature of 5–6, 16–17; domain-specific 11; epistemic 10; learned strategies 5; metacognitive 10; in problem solving and domain learning 5–8; retention of 17–18; state-based 13; surface-level 11; trait-based 13; "waves" of use 17; *see also* domain-general strategies
strategy use, measurement of: aspects to measure 108–10; concurrent self-report 112–13; as formative evaluation 114–15; observations 113–14; prospective self-report 111; retrospective self-report 111; semi-structured interviews 112; structured interviews 112
strikes 84
structured interviews 112
studying: attentional strategies 25–6; definition of 25; elaborative strategies for 29–31; generative strategies for 32–3; help-seeking strategies for 33; organizational strategies for 26–9; working memory strategies for 31–2
summarizing 31
summative assessment 114
surface-level strategies: definition of 11; for reading 41–4
surprise, expressing 48
symbolic strategies: definition of 67; shift from pictorial strategies to 77; types of 70–6
synonyms, as second language strategy 60–1
systems 94

tactical decision making 66–7
TAP (think-aloud protocol) 112–13
tasks: ill-structured 22; well-structured 21–2
teaching 33
text: agreement with 47; arguing with 46; evaluating importance

of 43–4; evaluating quality of 43; text features 42
think-aloud protocol (TAP) 112–13
topic knowledge 19, 101
trait-based strategies 13
translating strategies 57–9
translation, direct 60

underlining 25–6, 42
usefulness, measurement of 109–10

validation, knowledge-based 88
variables, control of 82–3
verbal protocol analysis 112–13
visualizing: appropriateness of 125; fractions 70–1

"waves" of strategy use 17
well-structured tasks 21–2
word meanings, guessing in context 41–2
working memory strategies 31–2
writing strategies 52–4; Cognitive Process Model 53; development of 61–3; monitoring 54–5; planning 55–6; POW writing model 53–4; revising 59–60; second language writing 54, 60–1; Self-Regulated Strategy Development model 54; translating 57–9

zone of proximal development 121